SOME LIVING
AUSTRALIAN
ABORIGINES
(Homo sapiens)

CRO-M

ROPEAN NEANDERTH

OLO MAN

RHODESIAN MAN

HEIDELBERG MAN

JAVA ERECT APE—MAN

NEANDERTHAL ASSEMBLAGE

GROUND APE

FOREST APE

—T.W. Voter

Meet Your Ancestors

By the Same Author

Meet Your Ancestors

A BIOGRAPHY OF

PRIMITIVE MAN

By Roy Chapman Andrews

The Viking Press : New York

1945

THE FINAL CHAPTER OF THIS BOOK APPEARED IN A
SHORTER VERSION IN *The Reader's Digest* AND IS
REPRINTED HERE WITH THE PERMISSION OF THE EDITORS.

PRINTED IN U.S.A. BY H. WOLFF, NEW YORK, N. Y.

Whatever is good in this book
is affectionately dedicated

T O

WILLIAM KING GREGORY
a profound interpreter of the facts of
evolution; an inspiring teacher and my
friend for nearly forty years.

CONTENTS

ILLUSTRATIONS

Endpaper drawings and text illustrations by Thomas Voter

PREFACE

ALL MY LIFE I have been a sportsman. Beginning with whales, I have shot big game and dangerous game in most of the countries of the world. There were some thrilling days but none equaled the one when we thought, briefly, that we had discovered a human skeleton, older than the Ice Age, in Mongolia. None of them equaled the excitement of unraveling the story of the Dune Dwellers, an unknown people who lived in the barren reaches of the Gobi Desert long before the dawn of history.

After the war many young men and women still will seek adventure. To them, I say:

"Go on the biggest and most exciting hunt of all—the search for the bones of our ancestors. It will give more thrills, and more satisfaction, than any other job I know, and I speak from a lifetime of adventure."

In the past, nearly all the discoveries of primitive human remains have been made by accident. We need organized, intensive search, using the modern methods and latest information of science. Go, I pray, to Asia or Africa. There is where the most important results will be attained. Both countries are almost virgin fields. If these pages inspire even one man, or one woman, to undertake seriously the quest, my efforts will have been worth while.

There is another reason why I wrote this book. Every thinking person would like to know by what steps he came to be what he is today and what actual proof we have. He would like to know, but seldom does he have the time, training, or inclination to read the technical, or even the excellent detailed popular books, on the subject of human evolution. He wants the most important and most interesting information presented in a concentrated and easily digestible pill. That fact I discovered during the past twenty years while talking with literally hundreds of people about the evolution of man. All of their questions more or less followed the same pattern. The basis of this little book is taken from those queries. For that audience, I have endeavored to present in *streamlined form* what is known to date, from actual specimens, about the physical development, home life, and environment of primitive man.

It has been a tough job to try to bring the dry bones to life, to maintain accuracy and give authoritative information. Technicalites could not be entirely eliminated, but I have reduced them to the minimum. It is, of course, very far from a complete story of man's evolution, which is long and involved. Had I attempted that, my original purpose in writing the book would have been defeated. I have given only the conclusions reached by the most eminent authorities, with as little as possible of the technical evidence upon which the conclusions are based. Moreover, only those specimens are discussed which show the significant stages in man's physical evolution. I have adopted Dr. Franz Weidenreich's recent classification of human types as the best present judgment of their evolutionary position and relationship. Several exceedingly important discoveries of recent years have radically changed earlier opinions and have not before been presented in popular literature. To that extent, and the account of my personal experiences alone, is the information new.

My connection with the study of primitive man has been only that of hunting for his remains. I have done no laboratory research on the specimens themselves. But for a score of years I have been closely associated with some of the world's most distinguished authorities in that field and have been privileged to examine the originals of many important human fossils, and some of the sites of their discovery, under the guidance of those scientists who have studied them exhaustively. I have, of course, drawn extensively upon the literature of human evolution. Dr. Franz Weidenreich's superb technical monograph, *The Skull of Sinanthropus pekinensis,* published in 1944, in which he discusses many other primitive human types, has been my constant source of reference for the latest authoritative pronouncements. To Dr. Raymond Murray's *Man's Unknown Ancestors* I can enthusiastically refer those readers who wish a more complete account of human evolution than the scope of this book allows. From Dr. William Howell's *Mankind So Far* I have derived much information, and of course Dr. Earnest A. Hooton's *Up from the Ape* and *Apes, Men and Morons* are classics to whom any biographer of primitive man is committed. Dr. Frederick Tilney's *The Master of Destiny* is a fascinating book about the brain, to which I have had frequent reference.

Dr. Weidenreich has been unfailingly kind. He has read much of the manuscript of this book for technical accuracy. My colleagues of the American Museum of Natural History, Drs. William K. Gregory and N. C. Nelson, have read those chapters which deal with their particular fields. Mr. Abel I. Smith, of Norfolk, Connecticut, gave me valuable advice in the arrangement of the material. To all of these gentlemen my best thanks are tendered. None of them, however, is in any way responsible for the deficiencies of the book, of which, doubtless, there are many.

Pondwood Farm, Colebrook, Conn.
May 1, 1945

Meet Your Ancestors

Neanderthal Man

CHAPTER ONE

Relatives and Ancestors

I OFTEN STOP for a moment when visitors are looking at the gorilla habitat group in the Akeley African Hall of the American Museum of Natural History. I stop because I want to irritate myself by hearing a remark that I know I will hear; it's like pressing a sore spot just to be sure it is still sore. The remark is: "No one can make me believe I came from an ape like that!" I almost never miss. Someone is sure to say it.

That Darwin said man came from a living ape is one of those fallacies of natural science as hard to down as the belief that whales are fishes, that the hoop-snake takes its tail in its mouth to roll downhill, and that monkeys form a living bridge across a crocodile-infested river by holding to one another's tails. What makes it so annoying is that science does not maintain such a thesis and never has. What it does say, is that the man-like apes—gorilla, chimpanzee, orangutan, and gibbon—are our *relatives,* not our immediate ancestors; that they came *with* man from a common stock back in the far dim past; that the ape-human stem early became divided into two main branches, one developing in the direction of man, the other in that of the living great apes.

Of course, the real trouble is that mankind is essentially snobbish. It does not want to admit that its ancestors lived "on the other side of the railroad tracks" and were of extremely lowly origin. Just because we dominate the earth now and are fond of "acting like the viceroy of God," it hurts our pride to admit that our great ad infinitum grandfathers and grandmothers searched for grubs under stones, hung about like jackals, happy to get the leavings from kills of the saber-toothed tiger and other carnivores, and had not very nice cannibalistic habits. A specially created Adam and Eve, dallying in a beautiful garden and eating apples, are the kind of ancestors of whom we could really be proud.

Doubtless our early progenitors did eat apples and fruit of all kinds, as well as berries, birds' eggs, and nuts when they could get them. But the teeth they left behind show they were omnivorous, just as we are. They liked meat. Probably most of what they got was carrion. Plenty of evidence indicates that two of their favorite dishes were brains and marrow, human and otherwise. It would not make the slightest difference to a primitive Benedict that the brains were those of his own mother-in-law who had bored him to the point of her extinction. The marrow from her leg bones would taste just as good as any other.

As a matter of fact, cannibals still exist and there would be many more if eating each other wasn't frowned upon by government. I have read that former cannibals say human flesh is delicious, but that white men are rather salty. I never could understand why biographers of primitive man raise their eyebrows at the cannibalistic habits of our ancestors when men of our own species now living, practice the custom. These tastes are just "hold overs" from our primitive state. Today, fried calves' brains are served at our best restaurants and marrow is a special delicacy. Some gourmets think Limburger cheese is delectable. It doesn't smell any better to my nose than a dead horse! The Eskimos prefer frozen rotten fish to the fresh article. Englishmen like their game very, very high.

But no matter what we would like to believe, facts are facts. There is incontrovertible proof that man and the great apes are not very distantly related and that they both inherited many characters from a common ancestor. Comparative anatomy demonstrates that our bodies and those of the anthropoids are built upon a similar pattern. Of course, the proportions are different. The apes have long arms and short legs, while with us the opposite is true. But their skeletons, teeth, muscles, and visceral anatomy are astoundingly like ours. Even their brains. The late Dr. Frederick Tilney has said that the gorilla's brain is almost human. The counterpart of each individual fold, or convolution, is evident, the only difference being that they are less complex than in man, who has the fundamental advantage of expansion because of a larger skull.

The embryonic development, the female reproductive organs and the unfolding of the sexual life, the reduction or absence of the penis bone, the reaction to drugs and to various diseases are remarkably similar in all the great apes and man.

5

Syphilis is a peculiarly human disease, and yet, inoculated chimpanzees developed both primary and secondary symptoms. In captivity, gorillas and chimps are especially susceptible to pneumonia and influenza. Blood tests are even more convincing. Experiments demonstrate that if the blood of a man is introduced into a chimpanzee a harmonious blending takes place. But if it is transfused into a horse or dog, agitation ensues and red blood corpuscles are destroyed. Biochemical blood reactions very definitely establish the relationship between man and the anthropoids.

Sir Arthur Keith found that only thirty per cent of man's structural characters are peculiar to himself. Among the remaining seventy per cent, man shares twenty-six per cent with the gorilla and chimpanzee, but with no other mammal. Professor Huxley rightly maintained that the structural differences between man and the great apes are less than those which separate the anthropoids from the lower apes.

OUR APE ANCESTOR

The main stem of our family tree goes back to a group of giant apes known as the "dryopithecids." These were the sort of beasts from which the gorilla, chimpanzee, orangutan, gibbon, *and* man probably developed. The genus *Dryopithecus,* or Forest Ape, represents an extremely diversified family —real apes, but apes with human possibilities. They lived in Europe, Asia, and Africa—going from Spain to India—during the Miocene and Pliocene periods, something like one

6

to fifteen million years ago. So our *nth* degree progenitors carry us back only that far. The early Insectivores, including the ancestors of the shrews and moles that we trap on our lawns and in the bushes, can trace their lineage to the close of the dim Age of Reptiles seventy or eighty million years B.C. We found the remains of these tiny mammals in the Gobi Desert along with the dinosaur eggs. Fifteen million years for our remote ape ancestry is merely a drop in the geological bucket. Instead of being one of the "oldest families," we are almost the newest comers.

But the Forest Ape never will make the front pages of the newspapers. If he is mentioned at all, he will be tucked off in some obscure corner of an inside sheet. No editor would feature an animal whose characters as a good "structural ancestor" of man can only be discerned if pointed out by a scientist. Especially since the teeth provide the most convincing proof. My colleague, Dr. William King Gregory, who has been studying teeth for forty odd years—and who, more than a quarter of a century ago, initiated me into the mystery of the "Tritubercular Theory of the Mammalian Molar Tooth"— is primarily responsible for establishing the Forest Ape as one who stood at, or near, the fork of the road where ape and man diverged. Dr. Gregory has shown that the molar teeth of the Forest Ape had almost the same basic arrangement of the cusps as those in many human first and second lower molars, in most fossil men, and in the gorilla and chimpanzee. He calls it the "*Dryopithecus* pattern." It is a consistent arrangement which, with modifications, has persisted through the ages and could not possibly be due to chance.

7

The Forest Ape was big—almost as large as a modern man. The teeth and fragmentary jaws are all that we have of him except a slender thigh bone which, in its form, suggests that he progressed through the trees by swinging from one branch to another. The gibbons, orangutans, and chimpanzees travel that way—"brachiation," it is called. I must talk a little about brachiation because it was of the utmost importance in the early development of man's erect posture. One genus of gibbons is named *Hylobates* (tree walkers) but they can do a good deal more than walk in the trees. When I hunted them in Yunnan and Burma they gave me the surprise of my life. The first time I saw them was just after I had returned to camp from inspecting a line of traps. Suddenly the forest resounded with the breath-taking call of the gibbons—*hu-wa, hu-wa, hu-wa.* It seemed a long way off but became louder and clearer every minute. Seizing my rifle I dashed down the mountainside, slipping, stumbling, and falling. The animals were in the giant forest about five hundred feet below the summit of the ridge, and as I neared them I moved cautiously from tree to tree, going forward only when they called. It was one of the most exciting stalks I have ever made, for the wild, ringing howls seemed almost above my head.

But I was still a hundred yards away when a huge black ape leaped out of a tree top just as I stepped from behind a bush. He saw me instantly. For a full half-minute he hung suspended by one arm, his round head thrust forward, staring intently; then launching himself through the air as though shot from a catapult, he caught a branch twenty feet away, swung to another, and literally flew through the tree tops.

Without a sound save the swish of boughs and splash after splash in the leaves, the herd followed him down the hill, fading into the forest like black shadows. The way they could throw themselves from tree to tree with unerring precision was one of the most amazing things I have ever witnessed. They could travel through the leafy tops much faster than I could run on level open ground.

Although wild gibbons seldom come down to earth, they can walk and run more effectively than any of the other man-like apes, because of their light bodies and proportionately long legs. Their gait is waddling and awkward and their long arms are almost always carried above their heads for balance. Nevertheless they can run with considerable speed.

The orangutan brachiates in a much less spectacular manner than does the gibbon. I followed one in Borneo, but never got a shot. He must have weighed close to two hundred pounds and yet with his enormous arms he could swing across the tree tops faster than I could travel through the jungle. Surprisingly enough, he never jumped or seemed to hurry. Running along the bigger branches, he could reach out for a projecting bough and swing himself across to the next one. On the ground the orangs are greatly handicapped by their extremely short legs. As a result, they usually travel on all fours, but can straighten up and walk in a sort of shuffling lope. "His walking gait has been likened to that of a very old man bent down by age, hobbling along with the aid of a cane," says Dr. Tilney.

Chimpanzees also brachiate in a way and are expert

9

climbers. They swing from limb to limb but spend a good deal of time on the forest floor. Although they can stand and walk erect they prefer to go on all fours, resting their weight on the knuckles of the fingers. I am very fond of chimpanzees, perhaps because I got to know one intimately. "Meshie" was her name and she belonged to my lifelong friend, the late Harry C. Raven, who brought her from Africa as a baby. Meshie lived, played, and slept with Harry's children. They treated her as one of themselves and in all respects she was a member of the family. He often brought her to the Museum where she lunched at the staff table with the rest of us, sitting in a baby's high chair. Her greatest delight was to ride the length of the Museum restaurant on her little tricycle, weaving in and out among the tables to the amazement of the visitors. She would climb into her high chair, sit most decorously while being served, and eat with a knife, fork, and spoon as well as any three-year-old child. As a matter of fact, her table manners were better than most children's of that age. Ice cream was her favorite dish but it gave her a stomach-ache if she ate too much. When I was Director of the Museum, if I wished to give a visiting celebrity an unforgettable time at luncheon, I would send for Meshie. A book could be written about her human-like reactions.

The gorilla is, of course, by far the largest of all the anthropoids and in some respects, but not all, is the closest to man. Because of his great weight he spends much more time on the ground than in the trees but swings by his arms as do the other man-like apes. Like the chimp, he prefers to travel on all fours with the fingers doubled under, but can straighten up and walk erect. His greatest handicap on the ground is his heavy body and short, comparatively weak legs.

Carl Akeley, who died in Africa while studying gorillas, was a militant champion of this great ape and often regaled me with stories of its human-like behavior. He made an interesting comparison of the measurements of Jack Dempsey, the famous prize fighter, with those of a male gorilla. (1923, p. 232)*

	Gorilla	Dempsey
Height	5 ft. 7½ in.	6 ft. 1 in.
Weight	360 lbs.	188 lbs.
Chest	62 in.	42 in.
Upper arm	18 in.	16¼ in.
Reach	97 in.	74 in.
Calf	15¾ in.	15¼ in.

Had a battle between the two ever taken place, it would have been an unequal struggle. Because of the gorilla's weak legs and clumsy movements, Jack would have danced in and out, landing punches at will. But even his hammer blows would have had little effect on a gorilla's jaw. It is doubtful that he could have scored a knock-out and sooner or later he would have been caught by a haymaker that no human could withstand. Probably it would have killed him, for a gorilla has three or four times the strength of a man.

Thus, we see that all our anthropoid cousins swing by their arms in moving through the trees. We are reasonably sure, too, that brachiation was natural to Ancestor Forest Ape.

*NOTE: See full references in Bibliography, page 245.

Moreover, it had an important bearing on the fundamental changes which enabled man eventually to walk erect on his own hind feet. The brachiating apes actually developed the upright posture while still living in the trees. Hanging by the arms straightened the body and produced internal adjustments. The head was always directed upward and the eyes sought the sky instead of the ground as in four-footed animals. But great size becomes a handicap to arboreal life. The gibbon flies through the tree tops because it is slender and light. The orang, on the contrary, tests each branch carefully before trusting his weight; so, also, does the chimp. Because the gorilla's body is much heavier than that of the other two, and his legs are disproportionately short and weak, the gorilla has fallen between two realms and is not well adapted either for life in the trees or on the ground. Were it not for the extraordinary strength of his great arms, he could seldom leave the earth.

When the group of ancestral Forest Apes began to increase in size they were confronted with the same problem that all the living anthropoids, except the gibbon, had. It became difficult for them to swing fast or far enough through the trees to meet the demands of food for an ever-growing body. They could find birds' eggs, fruit, nuts, leaves, and tender shoots, but the ground produced more berries, more fruit, roots, grubs, and a variety of crawling things palatable to their developing omnivorous appetites. Moreover, sleeping in a tree was not too comfortable even though they made nests as the chimpanzee and orang do today. So to the ground they went.

The Forest Ape found it to his liking. But to dig for grubs

under logs and stones, to catch insects or small running animals, his hands must be free. Thus more and more often did he stand erect and a new world opened before his eyes. To direct his hands, his brain developed, or the development of his brain caused him to use his hands; which it was is immaterial. The result was what counted.

At last the Forest Ape—the ape with human possibilities which the living anthropoids never had—crossed the Rubicon. He became a ground ape, an earth-bound creature, walking and running on two feet and sitting erect even as you and I. No longer did he resort to the tree tops when danger threatened. Instead, he sought concealment in the thickets on the forest floor. That growing brain of his impelled him to pick up stones; to hurl them at attacking animals or those he wished to kill for food; to use sticks and clubs. It impelled him to shape rocks and pieces of wood into implements for his use. When this happened he had grasped the lowest rung on the human ladder. It also led him by halting steps to explore the plains away from the shelter of the trees.

This radical change of habit, however, was not accomplished in a day or without a profound altering of his anatomy. It may have required more than half a dozen million years. Perhaps not so long as that. But what happened to his body is plain for all to see. The way in which it happened I shall not discuss. It would require a volume of its own. We are concerned only with the end result. Dispensing with the forelimbs in locomotion and their use as hands was made possible only by the development of a foot capable of supporting the entire body's weight. The ape foot was transformed into a human foot, which has lost the power of grasping, by drawing the big toe toward the other toes and later being tied to them by the shortening of the connective tissue lying on the web between the great toe and the other digits. It was transformed also by the increase of the supporting surface of the heel and the development of a plantar arch.

Dr. Tilney sums up the importance of the foot in the following words: "Whatever may have been the influences which caused certain members of the pre-human stock to desert the trees and live upon the ground, it is clear that one most important result of this change was the formation of the human foot. The structure was a solid foundation for the highest achievements of organic evolution. It ultimately produced an animal capable of dominating the world. It was responsible for all the extensive changes incident to the erect posture—for the rearrangement in the shape of the body, for the squaring of the shoulders and the broadening of the pelvis, for readjustments in the position of the heart and lungs, for new provisions in supporting the abdominal organs, for a reordering in the relation of the eyes to provide for binocular, stereoscopic vision, for the modifications in the neck to suit the purposes of the most effective head movements, for the freeing of the hands so that they might become constructive agents, and above all, for impressing upon brain structure the effects of these many progressive advantages." (1933, pp. 298-99)

The "opposable thumb" made the hand a more effective grasping organ. A gorilla's or chimp's thumb cannot be turned inward to reach the other fingers, but man has developed a powerful muscle for just this purpose. No less profound changes were necessary in the trunk when it shifted from a horizontal to a vertical posture. The viscera had to be closely bound to the wall of the abdominal cavity or suspended so that it would not sag downward when the animal sat erect; the chest became broad and flat instead of deep and narrow; the spine was curved in the lumbar region and the sacrum broadened enormously to form a basin for the support of the internal organs and to make a more comfortable platform upon which to sit. Many other changes, too numerous to mention here, took place throughout the body.

Long before all this occurred, the Forest Ape had lost its tail. Likewise, in the living anthropoids the tail disappeared far back in their evolutionary history. Just why is not clear; probably because they habitually sat on their rear ends and the tail vertebrae turned inward instead of continuing the line of the spine. An animal as large as an ape does not need a tail as a balancing organ; neither is it necessary to keep off flies or to curl about the body for warmth, like that of a squirrel or a fox. But that some time in our extremely remote ancestry we did have tails, is evidenced by the human foetus which from the fourth to the eighth week shows a protruding portion of the spine that later becomes obscured by the surrounding parts. Moreover, Sir Arthur Keith says that there are vestiges of tail muscles in about ten per cent of dissected human bodies. Very infrequently a child is born with the rudiments of a true tail.

In the Philippine Islands, in 1910, a native was brought to me for inspection. He possessed a blunt bony tail-stump two and one-half inches long. Obviously, it was a projection of the coccyx, which instead of being bent under as usual, continued in a direct line with the spine. A local photographer had re-touched and extended the projection in a photograph to a pointed spike six or eight inches long, and sold the pictures to tourists like hotcakes. For years afterward they kept appearing in my mail as indisputable evidence of a "tribe of people with tails."

Man's forerunners made their bodily adjustments with incredible speed, speaking from an evolutionary standpoint. Possibly it was less than half a dozen million years. If that seems a long time, think of the horse. It required fifty or sixty million years for it to change from the little four-toed *Eohippus,* scarcely larger than a fox, into the magnificent thoroughbred of today. Man accomplished a far greater miracle in a fraction of that time. Hurry has always been the tempo of human evolution. Hurry to get out of the primordial ape stage, to change body, brain, hands, and feet faster than it had ever been done in the history of creation. Hurry on to the time when man could conquer the land and the sea and the air; when he could stand as Lord of all the Earth.

CHAPTER TWO

The Human Story in Brief

WAS THERE a Garden of Eden? Yes, if you want to call it that. But not only one—probably half a dozen or more. India, Java, China, Central Asia, Africa, and possibly Europe can each claim one with reason. There were multiple Adams and Eves, too. That only *one* human type developed in only *one* place was the prevailing opinion until comparatively recently. But it has been outmoded by new discoveries. Evolution does not work that way. It is not a one-track process. It operates upon many different lines, in many directions, and is not restricted to a single region.

The evolution of our ancestral Forest Apes took place in widely separated areas and not in the same geologic time—some perhaps as far back as the Miocene period, ten or fifteen million years ago; others in the relatively recent Pliocene period of from one to seven million years ago. The Forest Ape group ranged from France and Spain along the Mediterranean region into Africa and southeastern Asia. Possibly, too, the late Tertiary uplift of the Himalaya Mountains cut off part of the stock from those to the south. That was the assumption on which I went to the Gobi Desert to search for early human remains. In any portion of this vast area some members of the Forest Ape group may have made unconscious attempts at becoming human. Of course, their development progressed at different rates of speed in different regions. If I plant radishes on my farm near the forest where the earth is moist and rich, they grow fast and big. A few hundred yards away, across the road, the soil is dry and thin and those from the same seed take twice as long to mature. Moreover, they are always small or stunted.

So it was with our ancestral seeds. Some of them never did make progress, for one reason or another. They became only half-human before their line died out. Others had better luck and eventually reached a human status. But even after the goal was attained by slow and halting steps and they became men of our own species, *Homo sapiens,* the progress of the different races was unequal. Some developed into masters of the world at incredible speed. But the Tasmanians who became extinct about 1870 and the existing Australian aborigines lagged far behind. Even though we are using submarines, airplanes, and radios, the primitive Australians are still living in the Stone Age, not much advanced beyond the stage of Neanderthal Man.

GEOLOGICAL AGE VS. STRUCTURE

It is most important to appreciate this unequal rate of evolutionary progress if we are to understand why some fossil human types found in the Middle Ice Age, for instance, are not as far advanced as others that existed at virtually the same time. We cannot always judge how primitive a man was by the geological period in which he lived. His actual structural characters (morphology) are the best criterion, because, as I have said, evolution does not progress at the same rate of speed in all regions. It is similar to my radishes planted in different soil in different places.

An excellent example of this unequal development of our widely spread ancestral stock is demonstrated by *Australopithecus,* the Southern Ape, from South Africa. It represents just the kind of Missing Link for which the public has been clamoring—one which combines so many characters common to both apes and men that the best authorities were puzzled as to whether it was the highest known ape or the lowest human. Yet, as far as we know at present, the Southern Ape lived in the Middle or Upper Ice Age less than half a million years ago, and is younger than some other types that had become definitely human. We would have expected it to be very old geologically. Doubtless, it was one of those non-progressive branches of the Forest Age group that developed very slowly. Whether or not the Southern Ape was a direct ancestor of any part of the human series, it demonstrates that there *were* intermediate characters between apes and men.

The next step upward beyond the Southern Ape *stage,* represented by actual remains, is the famous *Pithecanthropus erectus,* the Erect Ape-Man, of Java. For the first time a definite human arrives upon the scene. A most lowly type it is, to be sure, but he walked erect, had a larger brain than any ape, could talk, probably knew the use of fire, and fashioned crude stone implements for his use. Probably we would call him a sub-moron if he lived today, but he was far advanced beyond any living ape.

An intriguing possibility enters into the human story at this point. We may have in our hands the jaw and three teeth of the Java Ape-Man's ancestors. Moreover, those possible ancestors were giants! A massive jaw found in Java and three enormous teeth from South China appear to be more primitive than any other human remains yet discovered, and to be definitely related to the Java Ape-Man. They suggest that the human family may have passed through a stage of gigantism before the type best suited to survive was arrived at by nature. But this can be only a hypothesis as yet. Perhaps further discovery will clarify the picture.

We know little of the Java Ape-Man's home life or his accomplishments, from actual specimens, because his bones were caught in the mud flow of an erupting volcano and carried far from their original burial. However, this is not as unfortunate as it first appears, for his story can be deduced from a closely related type, Peking Man, who lived in the Western Hills near Peking, China. There we have almost an embarrassment of riches. The history of Peking Man's life is preserved in a cave which has been partially excavated and some chapters are as clear as though they had been written on stone and left for us to read. The Java and Peking men were at least first cousins, lived at about the same geological time and were in approximately the same stage of development. So what we learn about one was probably true of the other.

TABLE OF GLACIAL STAGES, CULTURAL STAGES, AND HUMAN REMAINS OF THE AGE OF MAN

GLACIAL AND INTERGLACIAL STAGES		STONE CULTURE STAGES		MAN
RECENT		IRON AGE BRONZE AGE NEOLITHIC MESOLITHIC MAGDALENIAN SOLUTREAN AURIGNACIAN	(NEW STONE) (MID-STONE) UPPER PALAEOLITHIC (LATE OLD STONE AGE)	MODERN MAN Homo sapiens, Whole world. CRO-MAGNON GROUP Homo sapiens fossilis, Europe. MOUNT CARMEL MAN Homo , Palestine.
PLEISTOCENE PERIOD	IV GLACIAL Würm			
	3 INTERGLACIAL	MOUSTERIAN		NEANDERTHAL GROUP Homo neanderthalensis, Europe. SOLO MAN Homo soloensis, Java.
	III GLACIAL Riss			
	2 INTERGLACIAL	ACHEULIAN	LOWER PALAEOLITHIC (EARLY OLD STONE AGE)	HEIDELBERG MAN Homo heidelbergensis, Europe. PILTDOWN MAN Eoanthropus dawsoni, England.
	II GLACIAL Mindel	CHELLEAN		PEKING MAN Sinanthropus pekinensis, China. JAVA APE-MAN Pithecanthropus erectus, Java.
	1 INTERGLACIAL	PRE-CHELLEAN		
	I GLACIAL Günz			
PLIOCENE		(Average estimate, 1,000,000 years ago)		

Chart of the Ice Age Showing Glacial Periods and Cultural Stages of Primitive Man

After Henry Fairfield Osborn
COURTESY AMERICAN MUSEUM OF NATURAL HISTORY

Peking Man could talk—his brain cast shows that—and he must have had a language sufficient for his needs. He had discovered the use of fire and made rough stone implements. He ate meat and certain plant food. Probably he was cannibalistic.

The Peking and Java Ape men form what is called a "group." They must have had common near ancestors. Just as one cousin marries and sends offspring in one direction while another cousin's descendants travel to other parts of the world, so did it happen with the Peking-Java Man group. Dr. Weidenreich believes it to be probable that one branch of Peking Man eventually developed into the living Mongoloids. Some of Java Man's progenitors, on the other hand, went in the opposite direction and very possibly gave rise to some of the living Australian aborigines. The latter relationship is indicated by the Solo Man of Java, *Homo solensis*. He comes from a later geological period than that of the Ape-Man, is further advanced toward modern man, and is a logical descendant of the Ape-Man. His connection with the living Australians as a remote ancestor is emphasized by the still later Wadjak Man of Java and the Tolgai and Cohuna skulls discovered in Australia itself. Thus we have two probable lines of development from the Peking-Java Ape men group into two present-day races of living man, *Homo sapiens*.

But what of modern Europeans? Ah, there's the rub! We have no definite indication as to just where that line started or from what particular group it is derived. The Heidelberg jaw shows that its possessor was certainly a progenitor of Neanderthal Man, who was one of our direct ancestors. But that jaw is probably the oldest known human fossil from a

geological standpoint. Therefore, Heidelberg Man must have originated from some unknown offshoot of the Forest Ape family, which progressed very rapidly in development. It may well have been the same stock that also gave rise to the Peking-Java Man group. My own guess is that eventually it will be discovered in Asia.

Up to this point we have been dealing with fragmentary remains where the links in the broken human chain are few and far apart. The missing connections have had to be supplied by study and deduction from insufficient material. That has covered a period of something like three-quarters of a million years. But about one hundred thousand years ago the picture clarifies. Typical Neanderthal Man of Western Europe appears upon the scene. Doubtless he went through a long period of nomadic plains life of which we know little. But when he became a cave dweller, and his remains were preserved in the caverns and grottoes where he lived, then the story of his life is told in detail.

We see typical Neanderthal Man as an advanced human. True, his physical characters are redolent of his ape ancestry, but he is a well-developed man with a definite social structure, primitive though it may be. He has the beginnings of religion, superstition, or magic—call it what you will. He buries his dead reverently, depositing beside them choice implements and articles of adornment and food. Obviously, he believes in some sort of life after death. He has invented pressure chipping, a new kind of stone work, which in later years was brought to a high degree of perfection. He can make fire. He is able to hunt and kill the mammoth, woolly rhinoceros, the cave bear and cave tiger, the most fearsome animals the world has ever known. He can exist through the bitter cold and blizzards of a glacial advance. He is in all respects a man to be proud of in our ancestral line.

Long before the European Neanderthals arrived upon the scene, man had become widely spread over the world. Naturally the type varied due to environmental or racial considerations, just as the horses of Asia and those of Europe and America differ among themselves. But Dr. Weidenreich believes that all the humans between the Java-Peking Man group, on the one hand, and modern man on the other, belong to one general assemblage of Neanderthal type, which he calls "Neanderthalians." Among the Neanderthalians he recognizes four distinct groups, alike in general but distinct in individual characters. Rhodesian Man he puts as the lowest representative of this widely spread assemblage.

Neanderthal Man suddenly disappears from the Western European stage about twenty-five or thirty thousand years ago. His place is usurped by the first modern men, *Homo sapiens,* called Cro-Magnon. They appropriated the Neanderthal caves and proceeded to decorate the walls with drawings and murals, the initial human art. Until recently, it was supposed that the invasion of Europe by the Cro-Magnons was sudden, and their annihilation of the resident Neanderthals complete. But late discoveries have changed that idea. Now it is believed that the Cro-Magnons infiltrated gradually into Western Europe over thousands of years, absorbed, and eventually exterminated the more primitive Neanderthals. Probably the invaders interbred with the invaded, so that remotely Neanderthal blood is mingled with our own.

The Cro-Magnons were men of our own species, *Homo sapiens,* Wise Men. They have been called the finest physical type the world has ever produced. Of great stature, averaging well over six feet, magnificently proportioned, with big brains and handsome features, they developed the first art and the basic civilization upon which we have been building ever since.

Before I go further, I must digress for a moment to clarify an important point. Probably nothing is more confusing to the layman who tries to read even popular books on human evolution than are the scientific names assigned to various fossil specimens. He knows that *Homo sapiens* designates modern man. But what of *Pithecanthropus erectus, Sinanthropus pekinensis, Eoanthropus dawsoni,* and half a dozen others? They are all in the human family. Actually they only mean that, in the opinion of those who originally described them, they presented certain structural characters which seemed to separate them, in varying degrees, from the genus, or group, of modern man. Subsequent evidence may show that those differences are not as important as were at first supposed and that the specimen should be included in the genus *Homo.* But still, the original name probably will long continue to be used for convenience as distinguishing one type from another. For the ordinary reader, the scientific terms may be considered merely as a latinization of Wise Man, Ape Man, Peking Man, Dawn Man, etc. It is extremely difficult to express degrees of relationship, or difference, among fossil human types by zoological nomenclature. Since there is a perennial disagreement among palaeontologists, anthropologists, and zoologists, what is a poor layman to do? Forget it, is my advice. The matter is largely academic, anyway. For that reason I have avoided using the latinized names in this book whenever possible.

CHAPTER THREE

Searching for Adam and Eve

EVEN THOUGH we know that different types of humans evolved in widely separated regions, there is still no general agreement as to where true *Homo sapiens,* the men of our own species, developed. Each authority has his own theory for which he will fight like a mother for her child. Therefore, I am presenting a brief review of the various opinions as a matter of record.

EUROPE

For years opinion as to the place of our ancestral homeland swung back and forth between Europe and Asia. Professor Henry Fairfield Osborn relates (1927) that between 1823 and 1925 there were discovered in Western Europe the remains of one hundred and sixteen human individuals belonging to the Old Stone Age. Except for two specimens—the jaw of Heidelberg Man and the controversial Piltdown Man—all of them were types of comparatively recent geological time—probably not more than one hundred thousand years old. There are, however, stone implements, not to mention the lost and almost mythical Foxhall jaw, from England which appear to show that man existed there before the beginning of the Ice Age. Because, in almost a century, only a single discovery of early human remains (the Java Ape-Man) had been made in the whole continent of Asia and none in Africa, opinion naturally favored Europe as man's homeland. But since 1823 Western Europe has been investigated almost foot by foot, while similar explorations in Asia and Africa have virtually just begun. Therefore, the dearth of primitive remains in these latter countries is not surprising and proves nothing.

ASIA

In 1911, the late Dr. W. D. Matthew, one of the most brilliant palaeontologists of the century, read a paper entitled "Climate and Evolution" before the New York Academy of Sciences. In it he advocated the theory of the Central Asian origin of mankind, advanced in 1857 by Joseph Leidy, and summarized his belief as follows:

"All authorities are today agreed in placing the center of dispersal of the human race in Asia. Its more exact location may be differently interpreted, but the consensus of modern opinion would place it probably in or about the great plateau of Central Asia. In this region, now barren and sparsely inhabited, are the remains of civilizations perhaps more ancient than any of which we have record. Immediately around its borders lie the regions of the earliest recorded civilizations— of Chaldea, Asia Minor, and Egypt to the westward, of India to the south, of China to the east. From this region came the successive invasions which overflowed Europe in prehistoric, classical and medieval times, each tribe pressing on the borders of those beyond it and in its turn being pressed on from behind. The whole history of India is similar,—of successive invasions pouring down from the north. In the Chinese Empire, the invasions came from the west. In North America, the course of migration was from Alaska, spreading fan-wise to the south and southeast and continuing down along the flanks of the Cordilleras to the farthest extremity of South America." (1915)

Matthew included in his general thesis the idea that the least progressive types of mammals are constantly being thrust out from the center of dispersal and the most vigorous continue their evolution near the place of origin. Therefore, he would expect to find the most primitive humans and other mammals farthest from the original homeland. Into this picture the Java Ape-Man, the only early human known from Asia at that time, fitted perfectly as did the non-progressive marsupials of Australia. Dr. Matthew's theory has found wide acceptance among palaeontologists, yet Harvard's distinguished Professor of Anthropology, Dr. Earnest A. Hooton, disagrees with it entirely. In fact, he goes so far as to say it is "altogether nonsensical."

Be that as it may, Professor Henry Fairfield Osborn, who very greatly influenced my own thought and life, never wavered from his belief in a human Asiatic homeland which he had announced in 1890. I was inspired by him to organize the Central Asiatic Expeditions in the early 1920's to test the theory. We had before us a completely unexplored region, scientifically, when we entered the Gobi Desert. Where we started work was mostly a matter of chance. We happened at first to go to the west. There we made new discoveries of great importance in half a dozen branches of science. We found surface evidences of human occupation in the way of Mousterian-type stone implements, indicating that primitive man had inhabited the Gobi perhaps as far back as one hundred thousand years. We discovered a new human culture, the "Dune Dwellers" of a Mesolithic Age—midway between the Old Stone Age and New Stone Age periods. But we did not find what we so ardently desired—really ancient man. That does not mean that he is not there. The geological strata of the central and western Gobi, where we made the first four expeditions, are much too old to contain human remains; many of them belong to the Age of Reptiles. It was not until we began exploration of eastern Mongolia in the last year that extensive sediments of the proper age, Pliocene and Pleistocene, were discovered. Almost immediately surface indications of primitive human occupation became increasingly abundant. Stone implements seemed to be everywhere on the desert, literally in thousands. Since there were few caves in this region, the early men had to live in the open, seeking shelter on the lee side of the sand dunes. When they died their bones would be washed away or scattered by predatory animals. Therefore, our best chance was to find the remains of an individual who had sunk in quicksand or in some deposit where a gently flowing stream had carried his bones, finally to bury them in soft sediments.

During the summer of 1930, on one of our later expeditions, our caravan of two-humped camels carried the expedition's equipment from place to place, while we dipped into rich fossil deposits, only to leave them for the next season's intensive excavation. But politics rose against palaeontology. As a result, I had to abandon the exploration of the Gobi just when we stood on the threshold of possible success. Peking Man had been found in China, only a few miles from the door of our headquarters, and we were more hopeful than ever that his earliest ancestors would be discovered in the now barren reaches of the Gobi Desert from which they might have journeyed to the more salubrious climate of the Western Hills. The possibility of finding primitive human types, or at least evidences of very early occupation of the Gobi, is by no means decided. It is still an important field for research. I have faith in believing that other scientists will profit by our experience and give eastern Mongolia the thorough investigation it so richly deserves.

At the end of September 1923, Professor Osborn visited the Central Asiatic Expedition in the field. He was enormously impressed by our discoveries and the evident fact that the Gobi had been a great center of origin and dispersal for certain ancient types of reptiles and mammals which later migrated to other parts of the world. On October 8, 1923, he gave an address to the Peking *Wen Yu Hui,* or "Friends of Literature," in which he stated the ideas which had more or less motivated his championship of the Central Asian plateau as a "Garden of Eden." He said in part:

"This brings us to the question involved in the title of this address as announced, 'Why Mongolia May Be the Home of Primitive Man.' We observe that early man was not a forest-living animal, for in forested lands the evolution of man is exceedingly slow, in fact there is retrogression, as plentifully evidenced in forest-living races of today. Those South American Indians who live in the forests are backward in development as compared with those living in the open. Of the latter, those living in the uplands are more advanced than those living in the river drifts.

"Mongolia was probably not a densely forested country—this is indicated by the animal remains found there in the earlier deposits. An alert race cannot develop in a forest—a forested country can never be a center of radiation for man. Nor can the higher type of man develop in a lowland river-bottom country with plentiful food and luxuriant vegetation. It is upon the plateaus and relatively level uplands that life is most exacting and response to stimulus most beneficial. Mongolia always has been an upland country, through the Age of Mammals and before. It was probably a region forested only in part, mainly open, with exhilarating climate and with conditions sufficiently difficult to require healthy exertion in obtaining food supply. . . .

"In the uplands of Mongolia conditions of life were apparently ideal for the development of early man, and since all the evidence points to Asia as the place of origin of man, and to Mongolia and Tibet, the top of the world as the most favorable geographic center in Asia for such an event, we may have hopes of finding the remote ancestors of man in this section of the country. However, this Mongolian idea must be treated only as an opinion; it is not yet a theory, but the

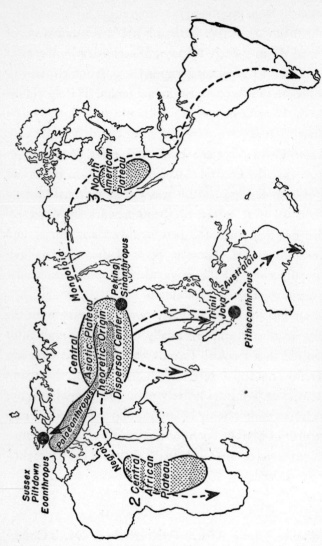

Theoretic Pliocene Plateau Origin and Dispersal of Man

After Henry Fairfield Osborn, 1929

COURTESY AMERICAN MUSEUM OF NATURAL HISTORY

opinion is sufficiently sound to warrant further extended investigation." (1927, pp. 163-64)

The brilliant Dr. A. W. Grabau is also a firm advocate of the Central Asian theory. He says, "Recent developments in China lead me to urge a determined search for remains of 'Pro-anthropus' the most primitive human. He should be found in the Pliocene beds of Mongolia and Sinkiang [Chinese Turkestan]."

Professor Osborn became more and more convinced in later years that the Central Asian plateau was an important theater of human origin, and it was a great personal blow to him when we were forced to abandon work in Mongolia. After his death in 1936, the new discoveries in Africa and Java were announced. These in point of direct factual evidence greatly changed the preponderant opinion as to the most fruitful regions for exploration.

Professor Hooton is particularly out of patience with the high plateau theory and is morally certain that man must have evolved in a tropical, forest area. Dr. W. K. Gregory, however, does not feel so sure, as does his colleague, that man's first attempts at living exclusively upon the ground was not in a savanna country with isolated groups of woods. From their excursions into the open for food, our budding ancestors could have retired precipitously to the shelter of the trees when danger threatened.

AFRICA

The discovery of the African Southern Ape, "Dart's Child," in 1924, and his public presentation at Philadelphia in 1937, brought another potential Garden of Eden into scientific consciousness. That this skull found by Professor Dart and that of "Near Man" which Dr. Robert Broom had found represented as near Missing Links in the transition stage between apes and men as we could ever expect, is attested to by no less authorities than Drs. Gregory and Hellman as well as Dart and Broom. These skulls, with the extraordinary Rhodesian Man and others, definitely showed that South Africa was an important field for the student of primitive human remains. Evidently, branches of the original Forest Ape stock had made valiant efforts to become men in that region. However, those so far discovered were not as successful in rapid progress as were their relatives in Java and China. But, again, we are confronted with the lack of scientific exploration. Where only a little work has yielded such important rewards, what may we not expect of a really determined campaign to prove or disprove Africa's claim?

In any "Garden of Eden," hunting for the remains of Adam and Eve is very much like looking for the proverbial needle in the haystack. Accident plays a big part. Most of the important finds have been made that way. Human bones are too fragile to be preserved as easily as are those of other animals. We do not find many fossil birds for the same reason. Then again, even the earliest men were more intelligent than the animals about them so they did not get trapped as often in bogs and quicksands where their bones could be fossilized. Neither did the great apes. Their remains are almost as scarce as those of humans. Of course, primitive man did fall into streams at times, or his body got washed in, and several important finds have been made in river drift deposits. But he was pretty canny about such places. If you put all the known specimens of primitive humans together in one pile it would hardly fill half an ordinary room. Only about four hundred have been discovered in a century. Some of the earliest types are represented merely by a few teeth, a jaw, or fragments of the skull.

Nevertheless each year more and more specimens of fossil man are being discovered and the gaps in the record slowly filled. It is a broken chain, to be sure. Many of the links are missing, and possibly always will be. Still the existing evidence pieced together, bit by bit, gives a pretty good picture of what our remote forefathers were like and by what steps in physical and mental development they reached their present exalted state. During the last two decades the discoveries of fossil humans have come with startling regularity. After the war I predict that intensive exploration will enter a new and brilliant era. We may expect an amazing advance in the knowledge of our own past history.

"How," I have been asked a thousand times, "does one search for human remains or fossils? How do you know where to dig?"

Well, obviously, you don't go out, stick a spade in the ground, and say, "Now I shall dig for primitive man and I hope to goodness he'll be here." You'd get a lot of hard work but not much else.

In the first place you must have the proper kind of rocks. Fossils occur only in sedimentary deposits—such as sandstone, shales, slates, or limestone. You would not have a ghost of a chance if you looked in what are called "hard rocks" such as granite, or any that have been subjected to heat or change.

Fossils are being made today, just as they were a million years ago. If we did not bury our dead in coffins or cremate them, but tossed them on the surface of the ground as do the Mongols, some of their bones would become fossilized eventually. Only a very small per cent, to be sure, but still some would be preserved. When an animal dies, perhaps the skeleton is covered with sand washed in by water or other sediments blown over it by the wind. These heap up higher and higher. Eventually they may consolidate into rock. Then a very slow change begins in the bones. Cell by cell the animal substance is replaced by mineral matter and the bones become petrified, or turn to stone.

Sometimes the bone is not merely impregnated with minerals but becomes an exact copy of the bone in the mineral itself. In the Gobi, I discovered a dinosaur skeleton projecting from a ledge of hematite. Enough was exposed to show that it represented a type new to science, but it, too, had become hematite and thwarted all our efforts to remove it. The rate at which fossilization takes place depends upon the amount of mineral matter in the sediments. It may be comparatively rapid and require only a few thousands of years. More often it is incredibly slow. Frequently we find bones in which the animal fats and gelatin have been lost but not yet replaced; these are called "sub-fossils."

Of course, the strata must not be too old. If the sediments were deposited before the animals for which you are searching lived upon the earth, you certainly cannot find their bones. For instance, it would be hopeless to look for the remains of primitive humans in rocks of the Age of Reptiles, when dinosaurs ruled the world, for they lived about a hundred million years ago. The earliest men thus far discovered cannot safely claim even a million years.

Suppose you have found strata of the proper geological age. It is useless unless a stream, ravines, or gullies dissect it so that you can see what lies below the surface. A frosted layer cake would be a good example. You can only guess what sort of a cake it is until you cut into it. If it contains raisins, the chances are you will see at least some of them. So with fossils; they correspond to the raisins in the cake.

A palaeontologist walks down a ravine or along the side of a bluff. A tiny point of bone catches his trained eyes. Then he begins to expose it. Perhaps that fragment may lead him to an entire skeleton, or half a dozen. I had exactly that experience in the Gobi Desert. While exploring a low sandstone ridge, I discovered a bit of bone, no larger than my finger, projecting above the surface. Carefully scraping away the loose sediment, I saw it was just the tip of a large, deeply embedded piece. That was enough, for I am too impatient to remove fossils properly. I called Dr. Walter Granger, our chief palaeontologist. He began work, not with a shovel, but with a whisk broom, a camel's-hair brush, and small steel implements. In a few hours he had exposed half a dozen bones. Eventually the deposit developed into a "quarry" where ten or fifteen dinosaurs had been swept into the backwater of a lake and their skeletons preserved. We worked there six weeks.

All because I happened to discover that tiny point of bone. It is an axiom that a palaeontologist seldom digs for bones unless he sees them.

But hunting for primitive humans is a somewhat different job. One is likely to have greatest success in the floors of caves or rock shelters. Even our earliest ancestors liked their comfort. It was much nicer to sit under a projecting cliff, or in a cave, and be dry and cozy when the rain poured down or a blizzard raged outside. Warmer, too, for they did not have as much hair on their bodies as did other animals. So they would appropriate a cave and raise a family. After the old folks died, their sons and daughters would stay right there in the ancestral homestead. This might go on for generations or even hundreds of thousands of years. Perhaps for some reason the original family vacated the cave. Another family might occupy the residence, or in later years even people of a different race might move in. Dirt, waste materials, and rubbish began to accumulate on the floor as soon as the first humans rented the apartment. You may be sure they were not very clean; no sweeping out was done by Madame, thank goodness. They tossed the bones to one side and slept and sat on what was there just like any other wild animal.

Even the earliest known humans used some kind of implements. At first they were only sticks, bones, or pieces of rock shaped by nature, and useful as tools or weapons. With increasing intelligence, they began to chip the stones into definite patterns for special purposes. The earliest tools, "eoliths" (dawn stones), are so crude that untrained observers would never guess they had been retouched by human hands. In later stages the workmanship falls into definite patterns called "cultures." These are surprisingly constant all over the world. These tools and flakes, bones of animals brought in for food, pieces of charred wood and the seeds of plants, mingle in the debris of the cave. The archaeologist digs into the floor with the greatest care. Every foot of earth is sifted. He notes the position and level of each scrap, or flake. He photographs, measures, and makes detailed plans of the cave and its surroundings. Like parts of a jigsaw puzzle each tiny bit helps to tell the story of that long past life.

Rock shelters were used quite as much as caves for dwellings. I remember, particularly, one such shelter near Beloit, my birthplace, in Wisconsin. It was high up on the face of a cliff overlooking the valley of a small stream. An enormous flat rock projected like a roof over a limestone platform. A dozen people could easily find shelter there. For centuries it had been used by Indians and as a boy I often dug in the hard dirt of the floor for arrowheads and bits of pottery. It was an ideal dwelling. Water and wood were only a few feet away, and if a skin were hung over the open front it would keep out the rain when the wind was from the south. As a matter of fact, a hermit made it his home for more than a year. He was a strange old man who lived by hunting and trapping and sometimes doing odd jobs for the farmers. I often used to visit him. His bed was a thick mat of dry ferns and he was as snug and comfortable as could be. Except for a few modern accessories, the life he lived must have been much like that of primitive man in almost any part of the world.

Ancient river and lake deposits are both fruitful sources

for the hunter of early human remains. I have often stood on a bridge and looked down into a shallow stream. I could see bottles, bits of china, tin cans, and bones of horses, dogs, and cats. These had been thrown in, or washed down from the banks by heavy rains and high water. Almost every lake or pond bottom today contains like debris. When the stream disappears, these objects will be buried in the sediments. It happened exactly the same way thousands of years ago, only the bones were those of wild animals, and stone tools or crude pottery took the place of tin cans and china. So the archaeologist always hunts for ancient river and lake bottoms when he is on the prowl for primitive man.

For example, I remember how, in the Gobi Desert, we found an archaic stream bed clearly delineated on the vertical side of a great bluff. It was easy to follow the course. We were looking at a cross section and could see the successive layers of heavy gravel at the bottom, small pebbles, sand and fine top-silt. At one spot there was an abrupt drop. Below, a heterogenous mass of pebbles and large stones indicated a pool at the base of a small waterfall. An animal that had been washed into the upper reaches of the stream almost certainly would have been carried into the pool, sunk to the bottom, and eventually covered with sediment. It was an obvious place to dig. In less than five minutes we located a jaw and directly below it a large skull. The place was a veritable quarry of fossil bones. Many animals were represented, but most abundant was a strange, semi-aquatic rhinoceros that had lived near the banks when the stream ran on the surface three million years ago. The deposit was too old to contain remains of primitive humans, but had it been of the proper geologic age we might well have hoped to find their bones. The words "geologic age" usually mean not an estimated age *in years* of a given fossil, but the "period" or age of the rocks in which it is entombed. These "ages" of the earth correspond, in a way, to such historical terms as Ancient, Medieval, and Modern. They are defined, not by human events, but by the great rock systems which occur in successive layers of the earth's crust. The use of the names of the different periods such as Eocene (Dawn period), etc. are necessary in any discussion of primitive men.

Estimation of the geologic age of a human fossil is arrived at by geology, by anatomy, by the stone artifacts found with a specimen, and by the associated animal bones. For instance, when a human skull is found, the inference is that the primitive man was a contemporary of the extinct beasts discovered with the skull. That seems fairly simple, but complications arise. Suppose the discovery were in a river bed. It might have happened that either the human or animal bones were originally buried in widely separated localities with a difference of many thousands of years in age. As the river excavated its banks the fossils were exposed, washed into the water, and carried downstream to be redeposited in a heterogeneous mass in various parts of the stream bed. In river drifts and volcanic mud flows skeletons are almost invariably separated and one cannot be sure how many of the bones are a part of the same specimen.

If man lived in the middle of the Pleistocene or Ice Age, that gives him an estimated antiquity of about 500,000 years. Of course, the non-scientific reader will ask: "How do you know it was half a million years? Why not a thousand?"

Well, if the truth must be told, no one does know exactly how old any geological stratum may be. When you are dealing with millions of years it is only an estimate at best, but still a pretty good estimate. If there is an error of a few million years in a hundred million, why worry? It is long enough, anyway. No geologist likes to assign a definite number of years to any period. He prefers to say, "It was a very, very long time ago." But that is not satisfactory to the layman. He wants to know what *is* a very long time: a thousand, a million, or ten million? It is natural enough.

Until comparatively recently the estimation of geological time was based on the deposition of sediments at certain specific places. For example, if it required fifty years for a foot of sediment to be laid down, by measuring the thickness of the sedimentary rocks one could estimate the length of time required to form those strata. But obviously this was not very accurate. Deposition does not go on in different places at the same rate all the time. Based upon this method, geologists believed that life on the earth began only about forty million years ago. But that did not give sufficient time for the infinitely slow changes in evolution which fossils revealed had taken place.

Recently a new, and much more accurate, method for the estimation of geological time has been developed, based upon the radioactive elements found in igneous rocks of various geologic ages. Dr. C. G. Abbot, of the Smithsonian Institution, explains it as follows: "Nature furnishes a calendar in the minerals which bear the radioactive elements, radium, thorium, uranium and their degenerated products, lead and helium. Radium, for example, constantly decomposes, yielding helium and a second temporary element called radium emanation. The emanation itself decomposes into more helium and a second temporary element. After five similar transformations the end product, besides the gas helium, is the familiar metal, lead. Such are the works of nature's time clock. The time element consists in this that radium loses half of its weight in 1,700 years, producing helium and lead at rates which are now well known and which no known agency can either hasten or retard. Basing their estimates of the quantities of helium and lead in certain of the very oldest rocks which contain such chemical elements as uranium and radium and on other similar data students have now come to a general agreement that the primeval earth's crust cannot be less than a billion years of age." (1930, p. 3) This is a very brief review of a highly technical process which involves an intimate knowledge of chemistry. If any readers wish to know more about the method, I suggest that they consult any modern textbook on geology.

The oldest rock analyzed radioactively gave an age of one billion eight hundred and fifty-two million years, according to Dr. C. A. Reeds. The specimen came from Sinaya Pala, in northwestern Russia. In a fascinating paper entitled "The Earth," published in 1931 by the University Society, New York, Dr. Reeds considers the age of the earth to be about three billion years and allots two billion years for the time since it attained its present size and outer crust as noted on the Radioactive Clock. He gives the length of the geological periods after the Age of Reptiles, to which I will often have to refer, as follows:

Recent ....began 10 thousand years ago
Pleistocene, or Ice Age..began 1 million years ago
Pliocene ....began 7 million years ago
Miocene ....began 19 million years ago
Oligocene ....began 35 million years ago
Eocene ....began 55 million years ago
Paleocene ....began 60 million years ago

Dr. Reeds has used an ingenious method to help us visualize what a very short time, in relation to the age of the earth, human life has existed, and how extremely young man is. He uses the face of a clock as representing the entire history of the earth. From twelve o'clock to twelve o'clock is three billion years. Each hour on the clock as it passes represents two hundred and fifty million years; from minute to minute fifty million years pass by. When the great dinosaurs disappeared at the end of the Age of Reptiles it is 11:45 3/5 o'clock and the earth is 2940 million years old. When the Age of Man begins, time on the clock must be counted in seconds for it is 11:59:38 2/5—just 21 3/5 seconds before the hands of the clock will again point to twelve. Four times in these next 21 1/10 seconds, periods of glaciation appear and disappear. In the 1/7 of a second we see man making great advances in knowledge. In the last 1/2300 of a second he is using airplanes to span the earth.

CHAPTER FOUR

The Ape That Almost Became a Man

THE MISSING LINK is a catch phrase—a sure-fire leader for any newspaper in the world. But not only *one* link is missing from the broken chain of human ancestry. Dozens remain undiscovered. Still, we have enough with which to reconstruct the chain pretty accurately. But the only Missing Link that interests the public is a sub-human, combining the characters of both ape and man. Just such a Missing Link has been discovered! Moreover, it happens to be old news, for the great event took place twenty-one years ago. It has always been obvious that when, or if, such a creature that stood at the fork where man took the high road and apes took the low road ever was found, it would make its debut unheralded and unsung. Its ape-man characters would be so obscure, so technical, that they could be discerned only by an anatomist. It never would fulfill the public's preconceived picture of the Missing Link. It would look so much like an ape and so little like a human that no newspaper reporter, no matter how imaginative, could stimulate popular appreciation.

That is exactly what did happen with the discovery of "Dart's child" in South Africa in 1924. His formal presentation to the American public took place only in 1937 at a meeting of the Philadelphia Academy of Natural Sciences where some of the foremost authorities of the world had gathered to discuss early man. But his ascent to immortality was accompanied by no popular acclaim. No flaring newspaper headlines proclaimed him as the Missing Link. No scientific war raged about his fragile skull; no friendships were broken in his name. The man-in-the-street read his paper in the subway on that eventful morning, attended to the routine of his office and ate his dinner that night, all unaware that the scientific goal of a century had been attained; that *the* Missing Link had been found at last.

There is an interesting story in the discovery of this Missing Link. It began with a child, "Dart's child," so called, for Professor Raymond Dart was the one who first adopted and christened it *Australopithecus africanus* (African Southern Ape). The fact that it was a child, that it had reached only the tender age of six years, was partly responsible for its long-delayed recognition. As an infant there were no other subhuman fossils with which it could be compared. Even gorillas and chimpanzees and orangutans of that exact age were hard to find. Yet its skull was the best preserved specimen of its kind ever to be discovered. It is a tragedy that doubtless many skeletons of this priceless ape had been thrown into the lime kilns from which our child just happened to be rescued.

The story, as told by Sir Arthur Keith (1931, pp. 37-46), takes us to South Africa eighty miles north of the famous diamond region of Kimberley, to the district of Taungs, at Buxton, in the wide flat valley of the Harts River. In the Harts valley an English missionary, Mr. Neville Jones, who combined archaeology with the saving of souls, had found many implements of very early Stone Age culture which proved that prehistoric men had inhabited the Harts valley from the first part of the Ice Age up to the coming of the aboriginal Bushmen; a period of more than half a million years.

For two decades a company had been working the limestone deposits at Buxton for commercial purposes. Out of their excavations had come the skull of a fossil monkey which eventually reached the competent hands of Professor Dart, of Witwatersrand University, Johannesburg. Realizing that the Harts valley had been for hundreds of centuries the home of primitive men, he naturally looked with a speculative eye upon the limestone workings at Buxton, many of which comprised filled-in caves. Since one of his colleagues, Dr. R. B. Young, was bound in that direction on other business, he implored him to visit the limestone quarry and bring him other fossils.

Just at the time of Dr. Young's arrival, a dynamite blast had blown away the contents of an obliterated cave some two hundred and fifty feet into the plateau and forty feet below the edge of the escarpment. The manager of the lime works gave Dr. Young a block containing fallen fragments from the cave debris. This he transmitted to Professor Dart. In the mass were embedded two fossil baboon skulls and a molded piece of limestone, obviously from a much larger skull. It was the exact impression of a brain cast and in another block he uncovered the facial parts and lower jaw. The teeth corresponded in number and arrangement to those of a six-year-old child; twenty milk teeth and four permanent first molars.

It was evident from the first that Professor Dart's child was not human and yet was higher than any known ape—something midway between the two. For him it typified the basal ancestry of the human stock. It represented an animal closer to man than the chimpanzee or gorilla and probably near to the ape from which man descended. The greatest obstacle to a comparative study of the specimen was its extreme youth. Had it been adult, the determination of its position among the higher primates would have been fairly easy, for an excellent brain cast was there. The first question would have been, "How big was its brain?" The human brain greatly exceeds that of all apes. It has made man the dominant animal of the world through its remarkable expansion in size, complexity, and power. But to find how close Dart's child would have approached the human brain, had it lived to become an adult, was a difficult problem. As Sir Arthur Keith says, the crucial phase in human evolution was the passage from the highest anthropoid level to the lowest human level.

Of course, the brain itself decomposes and disappears with the flesh. But the interior of the skull acts as a mold from which plaster-of-Paris casts can be made. The brain leaves certain very definite impressions upon the bony surface. The convolutions show as great indentations and the course of arteries can be traced by grooves; other prominent features also leave their mark. Because the brain is covered by three layers of membranes and surrounded by a thin jacket of fluid, its details are not sharply delineated on the skull. Nevertheless, the main landmarks are there.

Sir Arthur made an exhaustive appraisal of Dart's child, not only in its brain development but in cranial bones and teeth. He came to the conclusion that in shape and proportion of cerebellum to cerebrum its brain might be regarded as humanoid, yet in volume and convolutionary pattern it is definitely anthropoid; that in the profile and full face views it is certainly ape; but that the teeth are more human than those of the gorilla and chimpanzee or any other anthropoid living or extinct. He summed up his opinion, at that time, in saying that Dart's child was kin to the gorilla, chimpanzee, and orang but also exhibited, in a greater degree than they do, features which must be counted humanoid. Keith's belief that, like most parents, Professor Dart was overenthusiastic about his offspring, was shared by many other scientists. Dr. W. K. Gregory, Dr. Robert Broom, and a few others were a dissenting minority; they maintained that Dart probably was right.

And so the matter rested for twelve years. The scientific world more or less forgot about the Southern Ape child and went about looking for older, and more satisfactory, Missing Links. But not so the homefolks. It was very much on their minds. South Africa *must* have a Missing Link. It became a point of national honor. So in 1936 Dr. Robert Broom, of the Transvaal Museum in Pretoria, took up the search. According to his account (1937) he began a study of the limestone caves of the Transvaal and visited several, discovering various fossil mammals but no primates. Finally he met M. G. Barlow, manager of the lime works and caretaker of the caves at Sterkfontein, six miles from Krugersdorp. Barlow told him that years before, while he was working at Taungs, he had seen many skulls and skeletons of the priceless Southern Ape thrown into the kilns because no one took any interest in the bones. He thought, however, that a similar but larger ape was present in the cave at Sterkfontein. Moreover, a Mr. Cooper who owns the caves, wrote in a little guide book to the places of interest around Johannesburg, "Come to Sterkfontein and find the Missing Link." A strange prophecy, for Dr. Broom did just that!

Dr. Broom says that Mr. Barlow presented him with three nice little baboon skulls and one of a saber-toothed tiger from the Sterkfontein cave. The following week he gave Broom the brain cast of a large anthropoid which had been blasted out a few days previously. In the cave wall Broom found a cast of the top of the skull and also recovered many of the other cranial bones and eight teeth, but not the lower jaw. He felt sure the specimen was closely allied to Dart's Southern Ape child and named it *Australopithecus transvaalensis*. Later he erected for it a new genus *Pleisanthropus* (Near Man). In a different locality he discovered parts of another, larger skull which he designated *Paranthropus robustus*. This, however, proved to be a divergent type, not closely related to the others, so it need not be considered here. For simplicity, I shall use the name Southern Ape for the group.

Broom read a paper on his new discovery at the International

Symposium on Early Man at the Academy of Natural Sciences in Philadelphia, March 20, 1937, where I was present. He summed up his momentous announcement as follows:

"There is little doubt that *Australopithecus* must be regarded as an anthropoid ape somewhat allied to the chimpanzee and the gorilla, and only a little larger than the former. In structure the teeth, however, differ very considerably from those of either the chimpanzee or the gorilla, and resemble much more closely those of primitive man—especially those of Mousterian Man. They resemble also in a number of characters the teeth of some of the species of dryopithecid apes recently discovered in the Pliocene of the Siwaliks of India....

"I think it likely that *Australopithecus* will prove to lie somewhere near the common ancestor of the chimpanzee, the gorilla, and man, and a little higher than the dryopithecids. Not improbably it will be seen to be a little way along the line that branched off to grow up to man. And there seems no doubt that it is the fossil ape nearest to man's ancestor at present known." (1937, p. 291)

Thus, in the carefully guarded phraseology of science, Dr. Broom announced that he had found the Missing Link. His opinion was confirmed as we shall see later.

Dr. W. K. Gregory and Dr. Milo Hellman, two distinguished authorities on primitive human dentition decided that the Southern Ape remains were so important that it was worth the long and expensive journey to South Africa to make a personal study of the specimens. Coming at the invitation of Dr. Broom and Dr. Dart, they were received with the greatest cordiality by the South African scientists, who put all the material in their hands without reservation and gave them every possible assistance. They were asked to make their own unprejudiced appraisal, completely disregarding the opinions of the local scholars.

Drs. Gregory and Hellman not only studied the specimens exhaustively on the spot but brought back with them casts of

Hypothetical Sketch of "Dart's Child," the Southern Ape of South Africa

53

all the skulls and teeth and later made their own restorations of the "Near Man." With Dr. Gregory, I examined the restored skull not long ago. He pointed out what an amazing mixture it is of human and ape-like characters. It has, of course, the very heavy eyebrow ridges found in apes and most primitive men, and a low flat forehead. But the projection of the face (prognathism) is less than in apes and more than in the lowest known human, the Java Ape-Man. Although the brain cast itself is about the size of an average gorilla (440 c.c.) it is better developed, particularly in the frontal region, and exhibits a notable advance in the human direction beyond that of living apes. Also the teeth and the upper dental arch show a curious mixture of human and ape characters. For example, the small, almost completely human canines and lateral incisors are combined with huge ape-like molars. The fundamental dryopithecus pattern is very evident in all three lower molars.

Drs. Gregory and Hellman have said that the skull presents such an astonishing mixture of ape and human characters that for a long time they were in doubt whether to call it a very progressive ape or a very primitive man. They conclude that the Southern Ape must have been at a commencing stage of humanity, before the tremendous distinction that there now is between the present human type of mentality and that of the apes. (1939, *a*, p. 54) And that in addition to its connection with the chimpanzee-gorilla branch, it may be related, and not very remotely either, to the orangs on the one side and to the human branch on the other. (1939, p. 368)

Dr. Gregory, in a lecture before the Associated Scientific and Technical Societies of South Africa, summed it up in the following words: "Dr. Dart concluded at that time that his form represented a long step in the direction of the human race; and I do not believe, after the most critical studies that my colleagues and I have been able to make, that any reasonable exception whatever can be taken to that conclusion. It is the missing link no longer missing. It is the structural connecting link between ape and man. It may not be the actual ancestor of man, because the ape stock was distributed over a very wide area in the Eastern Hemisphere. It ranged from Spain in the West to India in the East and through East Africa to South Africa in the South. So it is difficult to say at what part of this enormous range humanity arose; but certainly a bird in the hand is worth two in the bush. This is an actual fossil form found in South Africa; and it does, to that extent, favor the view of Darwin that man arose in Africa. We may, however, find somewhat similar forms in India. We have already found forms approaching the lower levels of the human stage, but nothing so well preserved or so near the human type as this priceless specimen." (1939, p. 45)

In the same lecture, Dr. Gregory gave an illuminating kaleidoscopic picture of what is known of the fossil ape record. He says: "In conclusion, we have this actual situation so far as the known fossil record is concerned. . . . What we actually find in the record is that in the early Tertiary there are no apes whatever. It is only in the Oligocene that we find a very primitive form in Egypt, which is known only from the lower jaw, and it appears to be that of the remote common stem of both apes and men. After this we have a long hiatus in the record. Then, in Miocene and Pliocene times, we find a great diversity of apes in India and Spain and East Africa, ranging over almost the whole of the Eastern Hemisphere, particularly in the tropical parts. Some of these apes seem to have the potentiality of man. Then we find, very late in the Tertiary, or more probably in the Pleistocene, this *Australopithecus,* which was certainly well up toward the human type.

"In the immediately succeeding periods in Europe and Asia again we find a wide diversity of the sub-human races. So that, taking the record as it stands, we have no reason to hypothecate a long series of beings because we have the structural stages and the fossil stages, which indicate that man was one of the latest products of evolution." (1939, pp. 49-50)

It would, of course, be too much to expect that all students of primitive man would accept *in toto* the conclusions presented above. This book, however, is not concerned with technical discussions or dissenting opinions. Drs. Gregory, Hellman, Broom, and Dart have had better opportunities, by far, than any other scientists for a critical study and analysis of the original specimens at the place where they were discovered. Therefore, I have no hesitation in adopting their opinions as the most authoritative pronouncements on the Southern Ape as the best Missing Link thus far known. Let him who disagrees produce a better one!

I regret that we know almost nothing of the body of the Southern Ape, except the skull. Superficially, he must have resembled an ape very much more than a man. Probably he walked, or at least stood, erect. That is suggested by the base of the skull. Also it is indicated by an ankle bone found by Dr.

Broom and described by him in *Nature,* December 11, 1943. His hands were free to utilize sticks and stones as weapons or tools and he probably did so to a very limited degree. Still, not even an eolith has been discovered in his cave. From his teeth it is evident he was omnivorous as are we. Doubtless he ate fruits, grubs, roots, and a certain amount of flesh. Since there were many broken baboon skulls in the cave of Dart's child, it is suggested that the ape-men cracked them open to get at the brains, as later humans almost certainly did. But his meat diet probably would not have been palatable to us. Very likely it included half-rotted carcasses left by lions and other carnivores. It isn't pleasant to think of our remote ancestors as skulking on the outskirts like a jackal while a lion made his kill. Nevertheless, there is evidence that most of the early humans ate carrion before the race attained the intelligence and experience to kill for themselves.

The Southern Ape, as we know, lived in the Middle or Upper Ice Age, about 500,000 years ago or possibly less. The fact that, as we find him, he is too young to be an ancestor of modern man has been advanced as an argument against his acceptance as a Missing Link. Nevertheless, his *structural characters* are more significant than the geological age. Apparently he was an attempt by nature to produce man in South Africa just as had been done at earlier times in other parts of the world. He was a non-progressive sub-human. Regardless of whether or not the Southern Ape was a direct ancestor of any part of the human series, he at least proves that there *were* intermediate characters in the jaws, teeth, and skull between apes and men.

CHAPTER FIVE

The Man of the Java Jungles

ON THE SLOPES of a volcano in the hot, moist climate of the tropics lived the Java Ape-Man. About five feet tall, with a low forehead, beetling brows, projecting face, and a chinless jaw, he seemed more like an ape than a man. Certainly not one whom we would care to introduce to our friends even as a poor relation! But when he leaped to his feet he walked erect! The jungle lay thick about his home. Palms, banyan, teak, and other trees we know today stretched upward toward the sky, interlaced with vines and creepers. But the Ape-Man had as neighbors some animals that centuries ago faded into the limbo of Java's long dead past. There was a curious beast called a chalicothere, with a long neck, a small horse-like head, the body of a tapir, legs long in front and short behind, and feet bearing enormous claws instead of hoofs: an animal that looks as though he had been made of spare parts left over when other creatures were constructed. He moved with a clumsy gait, carrying his claws sidewise as he walked. In spite of his size he was a shy, defenseless animal, hiding in the thickest jungle. The tapir of the Ape-Man's time was as big as a dray horse. There was an enormous tortoise, too, with a shell seven feet long and weighing nearly two tons. We can imagine the Ape-Man sitting on the banks of the Solo River, watching a hippopotamus lying in the water with only the top of its head exposed, or sunning itself on a sandy beach. We can see him in the jungle, slipping from tree to tree, following a herd of *Stegodon,* primitive elephants, hoping to find one that had died or been killed in combat. That meant food for him. Carrion, it might be, but he liked his meat "high." It helped to vary his diet of fruit, nuts, berries, mice, grubs, and roots. In the trees he saw great orangutans swinging among the branches. Perhaps he looked with a speculative eye upon their clumsy antics. He might have pondered, had he known anything about evolution, something like this: "Once upon a time, long, long ago, my ancestors were apes, even as you. But now, behold, I have become a man! Not much of a man, I will admit, but still I am definitely human. I walk and run erect; I use my hands, I have a bigger and better brain than you. I can reason, profit by experience, and I've got imagination. Of course, not too much of any of these faculties, but still I do have some. And, most of all, I can talk. The rest of you can only make guttural sounds. Certainly they have meanings. You make the same noise when you are frightened, angry, or want food. But all animals can do that. Perhaps you are better than any others. Still, it isn't speech. You can't communicate your ideas in spoken words and I can. Oh yes, I have definitely become a man." And so with an arrogant lift of his shoulders, he probably strode off into the dim shadows of the jungle, to be lost to sight for half a million years.

But it was not the end of the Java Ape-Man. Fate, chance, or whatever you wish to call it, had marked him for greater things. All unsuspecting, he became the most famous and most discussed member of the early human family. He was destined to fill a vacant niche in the Hall of Fame of Human

Java Ape-Man Teasing a Giant Tortoise

After A. A. Jansson
COURTESY OF THE AMERICAN MUSEUM OF NATURAL HISTORY

Evolution. Beneath his bust are carved in letters of enduring stone, the words: "The Earliest Known Man."

When, half a million years ago, the Java Ape-Man lay down to die upon a sunny bluff where his dimming eyes could look across the waves of swaying jungle, his mortal remains did not crumble into dust. They were caught in the mud flow from an erupting volcano and came to rest on the banks of the Solo River. The flesh dropped away and the skeleton separated, but part of his precious cranium remained intact. It was reverently covered by a blanket of protecting sediments. Eventually the skull was fossilized, "turned to stone." There it lay until 1891. In that year it was discovered by a Dutch scientist, only to be reincarcerated for a quarter of a century in Holland— a strange chapter in the history of human evolution.

In 1887 a young Dutch anatomist, the late Eugene Dubois, became interested in the problem of the origin of man. He was stimulated by the controversy then raging in Europe over the discovery of several skulls of Neanderthal Man. For some unknown reason, he decided that the Dutch East Indies was a likely place in which to search for primitive human remains. So he got himself appointed Health Officer in the Dutch Colonial Service and left Holland with the avowed intention of finding an early type of man. And, by George, he did! It is one of the few cases on record of a scientist making good so completely in such an exploration.

Near Trinil, where the Solo River was cutting its way through an area of volcanic tuff, cemented with clay and sand into soft rock, many fossil bones of extinct animals had been found. Dubois, at his own request, was sent to examine the deposits. It was a brilliant decision, for in 1890 he found a fragment of a human lower jaw at Kedung Brubus; and at Trinil, some distance away, in 1891-92 he discovered the skull cap, a lower jaw, two molar teeth, a premolar, and a thigh bone, or femur, of a great man-like animal. The specimens were not actually lying together but were within a few feet of each other. Only the femur was about fifty feet away. All, however, were in the same geological horizon. The thigh bone is still the subject of controversy, some students maintaining that it has no relation to the skull. Many years later Dubois found in his Trinil collections four other femora, all of which he believed represent the Ape-Man. But this is by no means a generally accepted opinion.

This creature Dr. Dubois named *Pithecanthropus erectus,* considering it as "a link connecting together Apes and Man." With the human remains he found fossil animals of many kinds, including extinct species of rhinoceros, pig, lion, hyena, hippopotamus, and an elephant, *Stegodon.* These are very important, for they help identify the deposit as Pleistocene. Most authorities now put the Trinil beds as mid-Pleistocene, but there has been considerable discussion as to their geologic age.

Dubois returned to Europe in 1895. Then the trouble began. While there was no question as to the value of his find, he became the target for the arrows of scientists who did not accept his opinions. In the first place, they argued, it was by no means certain that the skull cap, jaw, teeth, and femur belonged to the same individual; particularly they questioned the last because it lay fifty feet away from the other bones and it was a mud-flow deposit. In the second place, said his critics, it might well be an "ape monstrosity," not a normally developed creature, and have no definite human relationship. Of course, the religious issue came very much to the fore. Orthodox churchmen were outraged. Adam was our first ancestor, said they, and he lived only 4004 years before Christ. Dr. John Lightfoot, Chancellor of Cambridge University in England, even announced the day and hour of his birth as "October 23, at nine o'clock in the morning." To maintain that this Java creature had anything to do with man was heresy!

But the champions of the Ape-Man went just as far in the other direction. They stated positively just where he fitted into the human picture, what he looked like, the color of his skin, how much hair he had on his body, and what he ate for breakfast!

Whether it was because of religious or scientific criticism or for other reasons, only Dr. Dubois knew, but anyway he took his specimens "off the market" and locked them in strong boxes in the Teyler Museum, Haarlem, his home town in Holland. For twenty-eight years they remained incommunicado. In spite of repeated requests, no one was allowed to see them. Professor Henry Fairfield Osborn told me how he, for one, discussed the matter with the President of the Dutch Academy of Sciences in Holland. He pointed out that Dubois was like an astronomer who by means of a secret telescope had discovered a new planet of vast importance in the Celestial Universe, and that this man then refused to allow any other astronomer to look through his telescope and the world had to accept his opinions, alone, in regard to his discovery. The President of the Academy promised Professor Osborn that he would try to induce Dr. Dubois to abandon his unscientific attitude. Whether or not Professor Osborn's great prestige won the day, I do not know, but in 1923 the distinguished anthropologist, the late Dr. Ales Hrdlicka of the Smithsonian Institution, was allowed to see the specimens. Upon his arrival in London, Sir A. Smith-Woodward handed him a telegram from Dr. Dubois inviting him to the Teyler Museum where he would be shown all the originals. Dr. Hrdlicka says:

"It was the first time the precious specimens were shown to a scientific man after their long seclusion. We found Professor Dubois a big-bodied and big-hearted man, who received us with cordial simplicity. He had all the specimens in his possession brought out from the strong boxes in which they are kept, demonstrated them to us personally, and then permitted me to handle them to my satisfaction." (1930, p. 45)

Professor McGregor, of Columbia University, also made a pilgrimage to Haarlem where he examined the specimens that same summer, and they were demonstrated on other occasions, including the XXI International Congress of Americanists at the Hague, in 1924.

All information concerning the Java Ape-Man rested on Dubois' specimens until 1931. Then the Geological Survey of the Netherlands Indies started excavations on the terraces of the Solo River near Ngandong, a few miles below Trinil. Eleven skulls and fragments of a much later human type were found and named *Homo solensis*. In 1936 an energetic young German, Dr. R. von Koenigswald, was subsidized by the Carnegie Institution of Washington, and began to search the localities that had yielded fossils similar to those of the Trinil horizon. A region called Sangiran, west of Trinil, drained by the Solo River, became a veritable treasure house. It was formerly a vast dome which, by a collapse in the center, had exposed the Trinil formations around the inner slopes of the whole circumference. In 1937 he discovered the fragment of a lower jaw of the Ape-Man with four teeth still in place. Another site, older than the Trinil beds, near Surabaya, the year before had produced the skull of an infant, the "Modjokerto child," which appears to be the Ape-Man's great grandfather's offspring. From still another deposit came a brain case, evidently that of a male, with some of the basal parts preserved. Dr. Weidenreich remarks that "it resembled Dubois' original skull cap as one egg does another." (1940 *a*) In 1938 the Sangiran district yielded the skull fragment of a young individual which further demonstrated the close relationship of Java Ape-Man and Peking Man. Another discovery followed quickly. Dr. Weidenreich tells the story as follows:

"The latest and most important find of *Pithecanthropus* was made in January 1939. The circumstances of this discovery are so exciting and moreover suggest so strongly the possibility of further success in exploring this area that I think it justifiable to tell the story.

"Dr. von Koenigswald had decided to go to Peking to study with me the *Pithecanthropus* material at the Cenozoic Research Laboratory, the best equipped place nearest to him. Some days before he left Java, one of the collectors sent him a jaw which in spite of being covered with a thick coat of matrix, was recognized immediately by von Koenigswald as an upper jaw of a giant ape or Java Man. Since the breakage was fresh, he instructed the collector to return at once to the site where the jaw was found and look for the pertaining skull. The collector did this, recovered the skull, and sent it to Peking.

"After preparation it turned out that the skull consisted of the posterior three-quarters of the brain case including the base, while the entire frontal region and the face were missing except for the upper jaw referred to above. The skull shows a wide cleft which passes through both cap and base in an oblique direction from in front and right, behind and left. The direction of the cleft, the straight lines of breakage and the smoothness of the margins of the split bones raises the suspicion that the crack may have been brought about by either a stone accidently shaped like an ax or even possibly an implement." (1940 *a*)

All the scientific world was thrilled by the new discoveries except Dr. Dubois. Perhaps the strange ideas that had made him incarcerate the original specimens in Holland for more than a quarter of a century influenced him again. At any rate, he violently contested the Ape-Man character of the finds and even did his utmost to discredit von Koenigswald and undermine his work. But he was unsuccessful and the exploration went on. In 1941 a fragment of a giant lower jaw with three teeth in place was discovered. This is an extraordinary specimen. Dr. Weidenreich has studied a cast at the American Museum. I examined the reconstructed jaw with him and was amazed at its size and massiveness. I tell its story in the next chapter.

So much for the history of our Ape-Man's discovery. Now let us consider the creature himself and the place he occupies in the story of human evolution. The thigh bone was an important part of the original find. A heated controversy is still raging over our poor Ape-Man's leg. Some scientists maintain that it belongs with the skull and teeth; others believe it does not. If it really is a part of the Ape-Man, it shows that he walked erect. If not, there is no reason to suppose that he stood on two feet. So runs the argument.

The discussion is relatively beside the point, however, because the exhuming of Peking Man in China almost certainly settled the question of his posture. The two gentlemen are contemporaries, very closely related and in approximately the same stage of development. That wonderful cave in the Western Hills has yielded a wealth of material and leaves no doubt that Peking Man was a bi-pedal human. Therefore, the chances are a hundred to one that the Java Ape-Man stood erect.

From the skull cap, Dubois made a cast of the Ape-Man's brain. When this was released to the world after more than a quarter of a century, it threw a flood of light on the sort of creature the Java Ape-Man had become. Probably he had the mind of a child, but an older and more intelligent child. His brain is better than that of any ape even though it is sub-human in size. A large brain in modern man does not necessarily mean great intelligence, although the two often go together. Brains of unusual size are sometimes inferior in quality. As a matter of fact, the biggest brain on record, according to Dr. Frederick Tilney, belonged to a feeble-minded gardener in London. Folding of the surface and the complexity of its convolutions and fissures are more important than mere size. Still, size is a controlling factor up to a point. The modern human brain ranges from about 1000 to more than 1400 cubic centimeters, the average being about 1350 c.c. Below 1000 c.c., a man would be unlikely to have normal intelligence. The brain of a very large gorilla is about 600 c.c. That of Dubois' original skull of the Java Ape-Man was 914 c.c., but von Koenigswald's first Sangiran specimen measured 775 c.c.

Thus, they stand intermediate between that of the giant apes and the lowest living races in point of size.

Dr. Tilney studied the psychology of the Java Ape-Man by means of a brain cast from the original skull cap. He found that the most striking feature was the great expansion of the frontal lobe, by the growth of which, in his opinion, "the human race distinguished itself in creation by acquiring all that is in the title *Homo sapiens* (man of wisdom)."

"Compared with the brain of a gorilla, there can be no dispute as to the great advantages held by the Ape-Man in this part of the brain." He remarks, also, that the left convolutions are slightly larger than those on the right side, indicating the characteristic human quality of right-handedness. Moreover, he discovered "a well marked coil in the lower portion of his frontal lobe on the left side. In all living races this convolution is associated with the control of spoken language. From this specialization it is apparent that the Ape-Man had acquired the powers of speech." (1933) Certainly his vocabulary was very limited, but still he must have been able to communicate his thoughts in words with fixed meanings.

The line between true speech and mere sounds made to indicate fear, rage, pain, hunger, satisfaction, etc., is the fundamental difference between apes and men. Without speech no animal could become a human being. Anatomically, apes are able to talk; actually they never do. Man's more highly developed brain freed his larynx for speech. A Mr. Garner built himself a cage in which to sit in the jungle and observe the great apes. He became convinced that they could talk. But recent laboratory studies show that while they have means of communicating their wants, it is not speech. Cries and emotional noises of various kinds are emphasized by grimaces, gestures, hopping up and down, beating with their fists, and in other ways. Speech came into existence primarily that individuals might communicate their wants and desires to each other or to members of a community; secondarily, to convey ideas and abstractions. It depends upon the mental status of the user. Few wants and few ideas imply few words and little speech. Language is a further development of speech. It is a product of human culture which made civilization possible.

Even with such a poorly developed brain, judged from the modern human standpoint, it is highly probable that the Java Ape-Man used crude stone implements and knew fire. His close relative, Peking Man, we know did, for ash deposits and charcoal and thousands of artifacts were buried in his cave. This was a great advance in the human direction. As Dr. von Koenigswald has well said: "The invention of implements and tools and the discovery of fire must have had the deepest influence on the evolution of man. It marked the level which separated him from the animals; it raised him above the anthropoids. The implement in his hand is an inspiration. It is the victory of intelligence over brute force. He is no longer an animal among animals; he becomes a hunter, can make tools, learns how to build a house. And when his food is cooked he changes completely from an anthropoid to a man."

It is not strange that no artifacts were found with the skulls of the Java Ape-Man. The bones doubtless were carried off, by rivers of volcanic mud, far from the place where these lowly humans lived and died. In the Trinil level, some distance from where the Ape-Man's remains were found, small stone scrapers, points, and cores, from which flakes had been knocked off, were discovered. They may be too advanced for as primitive a being as our Ape-Man; perhaps they are the work of a later people. But eoliths, those pieces of rock which were so naturally formed as to be handy for tools or weapons, must have been used by early men long before they developed enough intelligence to shape rocks for definite purposes themselves. It would be the natural process. First to use rocks which were comfortable to grasp, accidentally made by nature; next to improve upon those designs. Judging by Peking Man's culture, I feel quite certain that further exploration will produce the lacking evidence of our Java friend's handiwork.

It would be gratifying if we knew something of the personal appearance of the Ape-Man and of his family life, if he had one. But we can only guess. Artists have pictured him with brown skin, half concealed by black hair, sparse for a beast but too heavy for a modern human. They show his head thickly matted with tousled hair hanging half-way down his back, and bewhiskered jowls. He is described as savage, dangerous, destructive, feared by all animals of the jungle because of his cleverness and mischievous curiosity; living in gangs like bad boys of the slums, fighting with his fellows, teasing and annoying jungle creatures too dangerous to kill. It is an interesting picture but purely imaginary. There is not a vestige of evidence to show whether he was blond or brunet, hairless or hairy, social or solitary. No, the matter must rest for the present on the few bones discovered in the mud flow of the Trinil beds.

It would be pointless in a book of this kind to do more than briefly review the anatomical characters of the skull and teeth which distinguish the Java Ape-Man. We are concerned with conclusions, not with the technical details from which they

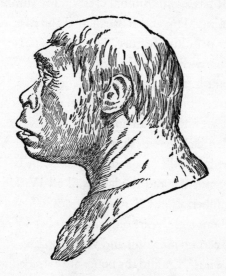

The Java Ape-Man

After Restoration by Dr. J. H. McGregor
COURTESY OF THE AMERICAN MUSEUM OF NATURAL HISTORY

were derived. In the Bibliography at the end of this book are references to publications which treat them exhaustively. Suffice it to say that, as one would expect in such a primitive type, some characters are more ape than human and vice versa. Nevertheless, the preponderance is definitely on the human side and demonstrates beyond a doubt that *Pithecanthropus was not an ape but a man.* The skull is quite different from that

71

of modern man in that it is small and low, with a very receding forehead which extends directly into the protruding eyebrow ridges. These continue straight across the frontal bone in a bar—a definite ape character present in most primitive human types. It has a longitudinal crest on the summit like that found in Peking Man, and is broadest at the base, not near the top—another primitive feature. The skull bones are very thick in comparison with those of any modern man. The teeth are more than half-human and the jaw definitely so, even though the chin is receding. His face is moderately projecting: about half-way between that of an ape and a man.

Dr. Weidenreich has designated Dubois' original find as Skull I, Koenigswald's first discovery as Skull II, the juvenile cranium as Skull III, and the last as Skull IV. He feels quite sure that numbers I and II represent adult females, number III a child about eight years old, and number IV an old male. The last has certain amazing and very puzzling characters. In the first place it is large and the bones are extraordinarily thick, so that in spite of its greater size the brain capacity is not more than the others; it is about 900 c.c. That of Skull I was 914 c.c., and Skull II 775 c.c. The longitudinal crest of the top of the cranium of Skull IV is not connected but consists of a chain of partially isolated knobs; the upper jaw is very large; there is a distinct space (diastema) between the canine and lateral incisor teeth, and a perfectly smooth palate. Dr. Weidenreich remarks naïvely: "I would have liked to pass over these disharmonies with the consoling thought that they are peculiarities of *Pithencanthropus* for which there is no explanation completely satisfactory in the present state of material at hand.

The discovery of the giant [jaw] from the Trinil beds of Sangiran . . . may, however, shed new light on this problem." (1943, p. 224)

"Skull IV," he adds, "irresistibly reminds us of the recently found giant human mandible, although the latter is still larger and more massive than the maxilla of Skull IV. The combination of a diastema and a smooth palate—features more ape-like than any observed before in hominids—together with teeth of a human character have their equivalent in that giant mandible of Java." (1943, pp. 228-29)

In the following chapter I have given Dr. Weidenreich's latest view of the specimen.

It has been generally considered that the Java Ape-Man was a side branch off the main stem of modern man, *Homo sapiens.* In other words, that he was *not* one of our earliest direct ancestors, who were completely unknown. Dr. Weidenreich, however, in his 1943 monograph holds the opposite view. For many years he has studied intensively the remains of the Java and Peking men. He has personally visited all the localities where they were discovered; he has examined the originals and no one else has had the opportunities for comparison and critical analysis which he has enjoyed. He is recognized as the most eminent authority on these early hominids. It is logical, therefore, to adopt his conclusions even though they may be challenged by some other scientists. Personally, I feel very happy about the whole thing. It is comforting to know who was one of our most remote ancestors and that we need no longer wear the bar-sinister across our escutcheons.

CHAPTER SIX

The Giants of Java

GIANTS DID EXIST in prehistoric times as living, breathing, human beings who loved and fought and ate even as you and I. That is now an established scientific fact. Giants stalk through the mythology of almost every country in the world. The Greeks and Germans depict them as huge man-like beings forever warring unsuccessfully against the gods. In the Bible account David slew Goliath with his sling. "Jack the Giant Killer" has been a favorite children's story for generations.

It always seemed to me that such a universal character of world folklore must have had some basis in fact—perhaps in legends reaching back into the far dim past, told in half-language by primitive mothers to their wide-eyed children. But my scientific training and a belief in giants did not mix. Science demands proof and there was no proof. Huge fossil bones and teeth have often been sent to the American Museum of Natural History, their discoverers hoping they had found a giant's remains, but we could only report them to be the bones of a mastodon or a whale.

Of course, glandular disturbances can make a giant almost over night, so to speak, and frequently does. I knew such a giant in Mongolia. He was eight feet tall and had a voice that seemed to rumble out of his shoes like the deep tones of an organ. I could walk erect under his outstretched arm. Moreover, he was as strong as an ox, which is not usually the case with abnormal humans. Once, I saw him pick up the Mongol pony he was riding when it balked at crossing a shallow stream, carry it over, mount again and ride away. The Living Buddha of Mongolia sent him as a present to the Czar of Russia, but the giant sickened for the open plains. So he was returned with thanks and lived out his life near Urga. His fame traveled so far that a circus "scout" tried unsuccessfully to entice him to America. I visited his *yurt* one day and met his father and mother. They were both of normal size. Obviously his gigantism was due only to an excess secretion of the pituitary gland.

A few months ago, I walked into the Osborn Research Room at the American Museum of Natural History. There on a table, with skulls of half a dozen other types of primitive men, lay parts of three real fossil giants. Not much of them, to be sure —only a massive jaw and three enormous teeth. But a jaw is a jaw and a tooth is a tooth. Half a million years ago, or probably considerably earlier than that, they were parts of living human beings. Dr. Weidenreich pointed to them with pride. A pituitary gland on the rampage could not have been responsible for the size of these giants, and they do not come from the same place or even the same countries. The teeth boast South China as their homeland and the jaw is a Java product.

I referred, briefly, in the last chapter to this enormous jaw found by von Koenigswald in the Trinil beds of Java in 1941. He recognized its hominid character and named the type *Meganthropus palaeojavanicus,* which means "Big man of Ancient Java." Shortly after its discovery, the Japanese occupied Java and cut all communications. There is no way of knowing to date what has become of either the jaw or Dr. von Koenigswald. Fortunately, Dr. Weidenreich has excellent casts not only of the jaw but also of the three teeth from South China. With him I examined the specimens.

The jaw is really awe-inspiring. Beside it the jaw of a modern man looks like that of a babe. In size, and especially in massiveness, it exceeds by far all known fossil or recent human jaws. In the thickness of the bone it is even bigger than the largest gorilla of any collection in the world. Nevertheless, the teeth and general structure prove that it is definitely human. The jaw has no chin and there is none of the abnormal bone structure which invariably accompanies pathological giants. Moreover, the teeth are correspondingly large, while in glandular giants the teeth do not show an increase in size with the jaw architecture. No, this was the jaw of a perfectly normal human giant. Dr. Weidenreich says, "It is undoubtedly a human jaw, but the features which render certain this identification reveal such an early state that they stamp this jaw as the most primitive human skeleton part ever found." (1944)

Discovery of the jaw led Dr. Weidenreich to restudy the big skull found at Sangiran in 1939, which he considered to be a male of *Pithecanthropus erectus* and designated as Number IV. He concludes that it is not a true giant form, when compared with the proportions of the new jaw, for it is neither large enough nor sufficiently massive. Yet in relation to the two smaller "female" skulls of the Ape-Man it shows a clear tendency toward gigantism and appears to be intermediate between Dubois' *Pithecanthropus erectus* and the type represented by the huge new jaw. In order to emphasize this intermediate position, Dr. Weidenreich designated the big skull as *Pithecanthropus robustus*. He points out that when considering the upper and lower jaws recovered from the Trinil beds, all four differ in size. Their structural characters show that the larger ones are in general more primitive than the smaller. Obviously, it indicates a group of related types, each derivable from the other in sequence of their size.

The Chinese for centuries have collected fossil bones and teeth, not for their scientific value, but to use as medicine. More will be said about this in the next chapter. Almost every Chinese drug shop contains a selection of teeth, and foreign palaeontologists soon learned that a careful scrutiny of the stock might yield important results. As a matter of fact, it was from an apothecary shop that the German Professor Schlosser obtained a fossil human tooth in 1903, which gave the first indication that primitive man may have lived in China.

Therefore, whenever Dr. von Koenigswald was in Hong Kong, he visited the chemists' shops. Between 1934 and 1939 he obtained three strange teeth, all of enormous size. The first was a much worn right lower molar without roots. Believing that it represented a new type of giant ape, he bestowed upon it the name *Gigantopithecus blacki,* Black's Giant Ape. The second tooth, purchased some years later, was an upper molar, considerably less worn, and the last a third lower molar from the left side, showing only slight wear.

Fortunately, Dr. Weidenreich obtained casts of the teeth, and completed a long and careful study of them in relation to the gigantic jaw from Java. He published the results in *Science* of June 16, 1944, and it is from his paper and personal conversations that with his permission the information for this account has been derived.

Judging by the degree of wear, Dr. Weidenreich states that the two third molars belong to different individuals. Possibly a third is indicated by the other tooth. The most important fact is that the teeth do not represent a new type of ape, as von Koenigswald believed, but instead are from giant men. In the most minute details they agree with the human pattern of the Peking and Java Ape men and even of modern man. Moreover, the form of the teeth is more primitive than that of any fossil hominid. Dr. Weidenreich says: "Therefore, we have the same combination which struck us in the human fossils of Java; namely primitiveness together with gigantic proportions. But in the case of *Gigantopithecus,* the gigantism reaches a new climax. The volume of the crown of the third lower molar is about six times larger than the average crown of modern man; compared with the corresponding tooth of the gorilla, it is about twice as large.

"In the Javanese *Meganthropus* with a considerable part of the jaw preserved, we can risk computing the probable size of the skull and the body. If a gorilla is taken as a standard size we shall not fail much in estimating that *Meganthropus* reached the size, stoutness and strength of a big male gorilla.

Concerning *Gigantopithecus*, we are more in the dark, because the lower and upper molars are the only basis for calculation. Nevertheless, it seems safe to say that *Gigantopithecus* considerably exceeded *Meganthropus in size and robustness.*" A big gorilla will weigh about five hundred pounds.

The condition of the teeth, and that of other animal bones from the drug shops of South China, makes it reasonably certain that they all came from the region south of the Yangtze River in the so-called "yellow deposits." The caves containing these characteristic deposits cover the whole territory, eastward even to the coast, and the fauna is everywhere the same. Similar animals occur in the Trinil beds of Java. For that reason it has been called the "Sino-Malayan" fauna. The South China giant is the human member of that fauna as is the fellow with the big jaw in Java. When the Chinese Malayan animals migrated southward into Java from the continent, the most primitive human types probably followed the same trail. This may have happened as far back as the Pliocene or the beginning of the Ice Age.

The hypothetical line of development is first the giant with the South China teeth (*Gigantopithecus*), for he was the largest as well as the most primitive human whose remains have yet been discovered; and he gave rise to the Java Man of the massive jaw (*Meganthropus*). His descendants in turn begot the Java fellow with the big skull (*Pithecanthropus robustus*) and from him came the classic Ape-Man, *Pithecanthropus*. Peking Man also may have taken his origin from the South China giant, only in his case, the development might have taken place on the Asiatic mainland itself. There is, however, not sufficient material to more than suggest this gene-alogy.

Another question is propounded by these gigantic humans. Was gigantism and massiveness characteristic of the evolution of man or was it merely accidental, regional, or individual as in other mammals? Another type of early human, *Solo Man,* which I shall discuss in a moment, as well as Rhodesian Man and the Heidelberg jaw, give some point to the assumption that gigantism was a general character of human evolution. But this interesting possibility must await further material before it can be positively affirmed or denied.

As a matter of fact, there is nothing so improbable about the existence of very large humans. These Java and Chinese giants lived during the Ice Age or earlier, perhaps more than a million years ago. Many of the contemporary mammals in various parts of the world reached their greatest size during the Pleistocene and became smaller in succeeding generations. The mammoth is a good example; also the "Irish" elk, the giant sloth, the glyptodon, and a dozen others. Possibly man's evolution followed the same pattern as that of lower mammals. Nature discovered that enormous size was a liability rather than an asset and that it threatened the existence of the type, so she cut it down. Her experiment hadn't worked. But that the giants did exist is certain.

What proves to be an important indication of massiveness in early human development was the discovery in 1931 by W. F. Oppenoorth, of the Geological Survey of the Netherlands Indies, of parts of eleven human skulls and two lower leg bones on the terrace of the Solo River near Ngandong, only a few miles from Trinil. One of them is colossal—much *longer* than any other known human skull. The deposit was very rich, yielding more than two thousand fossil bones. Among them were *Stegodon,* a true elephant, hippopotamus, rhinoceros, deer, and cattle. All the human skulls belong to the same type which Oppenoorth named *Homo solensis,* the "Solo Man." He is also called "Ngandong Man," after the designation of the fossil locality, but I prefer to use the former name. It is most unfortunate that in spite of the obvious importance of the specimens no detailed description has been forthcoming. Oppenoorth's two publications are only preliminary in character, leaving much to be desired. The skulls were intrusted to Professor W. D. Mysberg for study, but Dr. Weidenreich was allowed to examine the originals, and the Director of the Geological Survey of the Netherlands Indies presented a complete set of casts to the Cenozoic Research Laboratory in Peking. Unfortunately we have only the biggest cast in the American Museum of Natural History. No one knows where the original skulls may be or even if they still exist. Inevitably, Professor Mysberg's study will be long delayed and the results may never be published.

Dr. von Koenigswald says that although the skeletons of other animals associated with Solo Man were more or less complete, only one lower leg bone and parts of the human skulls were found. All of them have the faces missing, there were no teeth or jaws, and in only two of the eleven is the basal part of the cranium intact. He compares the others with a human skull that had been opened by the living Dyak head hunters of Borneo for the purpose of eating the brain, and finds it was done in the same manner. He says, moreover, that the male skull (Number V) shows clearly that the man was killed by a blow on the back of his head. He concludes that this explains the fragmentary condition of Solo Man's remains. "It is an artificial assemblage, a kind of primitive skull-bowl, either accidentally lost at this locality as the remains of a cannibalistic meal, or deposited for a magic purpose. For some time Neanderthal man was known to have been a cannibal in Europe (Krapine; Eringsdorf); now the same inference can also be drawn from the Ngandong [Solo] skulls. In this respect it is noteworthy that genuine human skull-bowls are known from the Upper Pleistocene of France and Spain.

"Only a few implements of Solo Man are known. The stone tools are primitive but the bone implements have been beautifully worked. A kind of ax was discovered, made of deer antlers, and a barbed spearhead of upper Palaeolithic type confirms the Upper Pleistocene age of Ngandong." (1937, pp. 31-32)

I examined the cast of the Solo Man skull with Dr. Weidenreich. It is enormous—a veritable giant in its own right. While it is by no means large enough to accommodate the great jaw from Sangiran and still less the huge South China teeth, nevertheless, it dwarfs all other fossil and modern crania. All the specimens are much longer and higher than those of either the Java or Peking men but they are most impressive in the massiveness of their superstructures and the great thickness of the bones; about twice that of any other known skulls. As a result the brain capacity is surprisingly small, ranging from 1035 c.c. to 1255 c.c. and averaging 1100 c.c.

Solo Man is obviously a very primitive type as shown by the flat forehead continuing almost directly into the moderately heavy eyebrow ridges, the well-vaulted occiput falling off abruptly toward the occipital torus, and the small brain capacity; also the maximum breadth in most of the skulls is near the base rather than the summit as in modern man.

Some characters show that Solo Man is a more advanced stage in evolution than the Java-Peking Man group, although he unquestionably belongs there, and the fact that he comes from a higher, and therefore younger, geological level, fits the picture perfectly. From the Java Ape-Man he inherited his general and specific features. Dr. Weidenreich believes that he is, to a certain extent, the equivalent or "opposite number" of the European Neanderthal since he is in a similar but more primitive stage. He cannot, however, be placed in the European Neanderthal group. Dr. Weidenreich believes it is not pure accident that Solo Man resembles Java Man more than Peking Man. They lived in exactly the same area but in a more recent geological period, and suggest that *Solo Man is the evolutionary step leading from the Java Ape-Man to modern humans*. He remarks that the size and massiveness of the Solo Man skulls are easily understood when we recognize the close relationship between the big Ape-Man skull (*P. robustus*) and probably with the giant from Java. (1943, p. 232)

It is necessary to speak here of another type of fossil man from Java. When Dubois first went to the East Indies, a prospector searching for marble brought to him a fossilized human skull found in a limestone terrace about sixty miles from Trinil. The following year, 1890, Dubois discovered another skull at the same place. Eventually these became known as "Wadjak Man." When Dubois returned to Europe in 1894, triumphantly bearing the Java Ape-Man remains, he said nothing whatever about the other finds. His strange mental reactions prompted him to keep the matter secret for thirty years. Then, when a fairly recent fossil skull from Talgai, Australia, was described, he calmly announced his discovery of Wadjak Man.

Unfortunately it is not possible to date Wadjak Man with any certainty, although he is very tentatively assigned to the end of the Ice Age. The skull capacity is large (1550 c.c.), the brow ridges strongly developed, the forehead moderately receding, the palate very wide, the chin weak and sloping. Most authorities agree that he is allied to the living Australian aborigines, but to what extent cannot be determined because of the meager account given by the secretive Dubois. Dr. George Pinkley thinks he is related more as a cousin than a direct ancestor, but Dr. Weidenreich says that the skull of Wadjak Man and those of at least some Australian natives of today are so near to the Solo Man that they appear in turn as advanced and correspondingly modified Solo forms. (1942, p. 65)

Two human fossils from Australia need to be mentioned in connection with the Solo and Wadjak Men because of their possible relationship to Java specimens. One is called the "Talgai skull" from Queensland, and the other the "Cohuna skull" discovered in Victoria. These men probably lived in the last part of the Ice Age and according to Keith are definitely of the same racial type as the living Australian aborigines, although much more primitive.

Dr. Weidenreich remarks that when the Talgai and Cohuna skulls and those of a modern Australian aborigine are compared with Solo Man, the likeness is surprising after due allowance is made for the further advancement of the Australian. He thinks that at least one line of development leads from the Java Ape-Man and Solo Man to the Australian aborigines of today. He makes it plain, however, that he does not believe *all* the modern Australians can be traced back to the Java Ape-Solo stock.

Since Wadjak Man is such an uncertain quantity, my chief reason for presenting him here was to complete the impressive list of primitive and exceedingly important human types that have been discovered in Java. We have the original Ape Man, Solo Man, the giant jaw, and Wadjak Man. All these came from a fairly restricted area in which only sporadic work has been carried on. Ten miles or more of the known Trinil deposits lie untouched. How many others of equal importance in Java and neighboring regions remain to be discovered, one can only guess, but certainly there must be many. I can think of no more fascinating or important field for scientific exploration after the war than in Java. To study these deposits intensively with the aid of the latest devices would almost surely yield rich results and add immeasurably to the story of human evolution.

Java is very young as an island. It only emerged from the sea at the end of the Pliocene, not much more than a million years ago. It belongs to the sphere of the Asiatic mainland, part of a larger Malay Peninsula. Dr. Hellmut de Terra has shown that due to climatic changes there were southward migrations of animals, and probably anthropoids, from the Siwalik Hills of India. More than half the fossil mammals recorded from the Java Trinil deposits are found also in the Narbadda fauna of India, even though these regions are so widely separated. Particularly significant is the appearance of the elephant (*E. namadicus*) of mid-Ice Age India, in both the Ape-Man beds and in the cave of Peking Man.

De Terra suggests that the north Indian mammals followed the tropical belt southward, traveling along the Burma coast ranges toward the delta lowlands of Malaya and South China. They reached Java at the end of the Pliocene period when the island had just fully emerged from the sea. He believes that the primitive anthropoids of the Siwalik Hills fauna were in a process of progressive evolution when they were forced out of their homeland, along with other mammals, by climatic changes. The necessities of travel and adjustment to new environment may have provided a stimulus to development, and it is to be expected that proto-human types would be discovered in tropical southern Asia (1937).

Thus, it is possible that the ancestors of the Java Ape-Man and the other primitive types originally came from India to the new and unoccupied island of Java, just as our Pilgrim Fathers migrated to America. It may also be that another group of the same stock made its way northward through Burma and South China and that their descendants settled in the Western Hills near Peking.

CHAPTER SEVEN

The Romance of Peking Man's Discovery

WHEN THE Central Asiatic Expedition first went to Mongolia in 1921, we became known as the "Missing Link Expedition" in spite of all we could do. This was because one of our objects was to search for the remains of primitive man, which we believed would be found somewhere on the great Asiatic plateau. Before we started I could be sure of hearing the same joke at least once every day.

"Why do you go way out there to hunt for the Missing Link? I see dozens of them every morning in the subway."

In Peking, the familiar American joke was continually in our ears:

"Don't endure sandstorms out there in the desert. I saw a Missing Link pulling a ricksha this morning."

Then suddenly the joke had a real significance. Almost at the front door, as it were, of the Central Asiatic Expedition's headquarters in Peking was found one of the most primitive types of humans known to science. The Chinese Geological Survey had asked us not to work in North China, as they were carrying on palaeontological investigations there themselves, but all Mongolia was open to us since they were barred from that region because of political reasons. It was very disappointing to me, for I had planned to explore certain deposits in the Peking area during the winter when it was too cold to work in the Gobi; thus my staff would be busy the year round. But it was a perfectly reasonable request and, of course, I agreed. We were guests in China and it would have been discourteous, as well as unscientific, to compete with their explorations. It cost us, however, the honor of revealing this important human deposit ourselves. We came back with dinosaur eggs instead of Missing Links! I would trade one for the other any day!

But to get back to the great discovery. It was made in the Western Hills, only forty miles from Peking. It stands as one of the most important known links in the broken chain of human ancestry. It is one of the most ancient. Of the early types it is by far the most complete. Its geological age and position can be most accurately dated. There are other superlatives which it warrants, but these I will relate in a moment. First should come the romance of its discovery and the well-deserved credit to its discoverers. Also it must be properly referred to by name, for even though it had been dead for half a million years, the christening took place only in 1927. Not again will the discovery be referred to as "it." "Peking Man" is the name. Scientifically, he will take first place in the list of distinguished dead as *Sinanthropus pekinensis.*

Bringing him to light was an international event both in

importance and achievement. Never before have so many nationalities been concerned with a primitive human discovery. The site of his long burial was found by a Swedish geologist, Dr. J. G. Andersson, accompanied by an Austrian, Dr. O. Zdansky, and Dr. Walter Granger, American, of the Central Asiatic Expedition. Money for the initial work was furnished by Sweden; later by the Rockefeller Foundation of the United States. A brilliant young Canadian anatomist, Dr. Davidson Black, organized and directed the excavation in conjunction with the Geological Survey of China. A Swedish palaeontologist, Dr. Birgir Bohlin, supervised the actual field work, assisted by Père Teilhard de Chardin, a French geologist, and three Chinese, Mr. C. Li, Dr. C. C. Young, and Dr. W. C. Pei. Dr. Black made the first scientific studies, and after his death in 1934 Dr. Franz Weidenreich, a German, continued the work. Seven nationalities concentrating their respective brains and different kinds of training and approach on one long dead gentleman!

Until Dr. J. G. Andersson came to Peking in 1914 as mining adviser to the Chinese Government, little scientific attention had been paid to the palaeontological wealth of China. Fossils were only of commercial value. The Chinese call them *lung-ku* —dragon bones. Like tigers' claws and whiskers, bats' dung, snakes' flesh, blood from a brigand's heart, rhinoceros' horn, deer antlers, and a dozen other similar ingredients, fossil bones and teeth were used as medicine. They still are used, just as much as before China was invaded by the Japanese. So they will continue to be used by generations as yet unborn.

When "dragon bones" are powdered, dissolved in acid, and

mixed with a liberal quantity of superstition, the concoction is supposed to be efficacious for every kind of illness from dysentery to bullet wounds. The apothecary shops do a lucrative business, buying their products from some lucky native who has discovered a fossil-bearing locality. In Szechwan Province, Walter Granger, palaeontologist of the Central Asiatic Expedition, found that the Chinese were mining fossils in deep pits. Some of the deposits had been worked for centuries, the rights being handed down in a family from generation to generation. Hundreds of thousands of specimens, scientifically priceless, had been ground to powder and sold to prevent stomach-ache!

Dr. Andersson, as a member of the Geological Survey, began a systematic investigation of Chinese palaeontology, the work being supported by Swedish finances. He encountered many difficulties. One of the most serious was the universal belief in *feng-shui,* the spirits of the earth, wind, and water which guard all cemeteries. In most thickly settled regions of China there are so many burials that it is difficult to find a place where *feng-shui* is inoperative. The fossil hunter must be extremely cautious in digging without having first obtained the consent of the nearest villagers. He needs unlimited patience, great tact, and a saving sense of humor.

Dr. Andersson had some amusing experiences during his first investigations. Once when he had gone through all the necessary formalities of obtaining the owner's permission to excavate a fossil deposit, his operations were halted by the sudden appearance of an irate old lady. Angry men are bad enough, heaven knows, but when a Chinese woman works herself into a frenzy, everyone hunts cover. This particular old

lady was so enraged that she seated herself squarely in the hole
the palaeontologist had dug, and refused to move. Dr. Andersson could not well shovel her out except at the risk of having
his face scratched; so, being a tactful gentleman, he tried making her ridiculous. It was a hot day and he borrowed an um-
brella and gallantly held it over her head while the onlookers
hugely enjoyed the performance. But the old lady only settled herself more determinedly and screamed even louder.
Then Dr. Andersson bethought himself of his camera, an instrument guaranteed to make any Chinese woman step lively.
He politely explained to the spectators that without doubt the
old lady would like to have her picture taken while she was
sitting in the hole. That was too much! Before the camera
could be focused, she leaped out, screaming with rage. But
even though she had been routed from her strategic position,
she continued to create such a disturbance that Andersson's
native assistants advised him to retire, leaving the enemy in
possession of the field until the smoke of battle had lifted.

In 1921 Dr. Andersson opened a small fossil deposit called
"Chicken Bone Hill," forty miles southwest of Peking in the
region of the Western Hills. On one of his visits Dr. Walter
Granger, and Dr. O. Zdansky of the Chinese Geological Survey, accompanied him. A native brought them a few fossil
bones from another locality and said he could show them
many more. The men accompanied him to the place from
which they had been obtained, near the village of Choukoutien.
In this quiet way was discovered one of the most important
spots in the world, from the standpoint of man's ancestry.
During the subsequent excavation Dr. Andersson found a few

bits of quartz which obviously were foreign to the immediate deposit. He thought they might indicate the presence of artifacts—stone implements shaped by human hands. Tapping on the face of the rock, he made his dramatic prophecy, as events proved: "In this spot lies primitive man. All we have to do is to find him!" The beds were partly explored by Dr. O. Zdansky and the fossils were later studied by him in Upsala, Sweden.

In this collection Dr. Zdansky found two teeth which evidently represented a primitive human type. One was an immature left lower premolar; the other a worn right upper molar, which he designated merely as *Homo sp?* The discovery was announced at a meeting on October 22, 1926, in honor of H.R.H. the Crown Prince of Sweden, who was then visiting Peking.

I happened to be in London at the time. The late Sir Arthur Smith-Woodward, the famous English palaeontologist, was lunching with me at the Berkley Hotel when the letter from Dr. Andersson was brought to our table. We were both enormously interested in the report, particularly because of its bearing on the Asiatic theory of man's origin.

But the world as a whole did not get very thrilled by the discovery of those two teeth. As a matter of fact, the newspapers, which usually seize avidly upon anything connected with Missing Links, gave it the scantiest space. A tooth, or even two of them, are hardly enough for anyone except a scientist to get excited about. Personally I got very excited. Those two teeth represented the first human fossil material, accompanied by certain geological data, that had ever been discovered on the

Asiatic continent north of the Himalaya Mountains. That meant more to me, perhaps, than to the usual investigator, because I had banked on northern Asia as a theater of human origin. I had banked on it to the extent of organizing the Central Asiatic Expedition and spending several years of my life in the Gobi Desert. More than that, it immediately recalled to me the remarks of the celebrated German palaeontologist, Schlosser, who in 1903 had described the worn tooth which he believed to be human. No one knew where that specimen, purchased in a Peking drug shop, came from originally. Schlosser pointed out that in the future we could expect to find some human-like type of anthropoid that had lived in China during the early part of the Ice Age.

Dr. Davidson Black, Professor of Anatomy in the Peking Union Medical College, was so impressed by Zdansky's discovery that he persuaded the Rockefeller Foundation to donate money to carry on the investigation of the Choukoutien deposit. An arrangement was made with the Chinese Geological Survey, which quite properly claimed the site, to work in cooperation, they to own the specimens but he to study and describe them. For the actual direction of the field work, Dr. Birger Bohlin was brought out from Sweden.

Operations were begun in April 1927. That was a memorable summer for those of us who lived in China. Anti-foreign feeling had burst into flame over all the country. The British Concession in Hankow had been forcibly taken by Chinese soldiers. Borodin and his corps of Bolshevik propagandists were directing events in the south. Chiang Kai-shek, in command of the Nationalist armies, moved on Shanghai. Nanking was looted and many foreigners killed. The Chinese, flushed with success, intended to drive all white men out of China. An officer of the East Yorkshire Regiment left Peking on a walking trip to the Western Hills and was never heard of again. A correspondent of the London *Times* likewise disappeared. News of foreigners being murdered came every week. A wholesale massacre was averted only by the prompt action of the British, who sent ships and troops to Shanghai. Eventually they were followed by many other nations. In the river at Shanghai was the greatest concentration of warships flying different national flags the world had ever seen in a single port. Altogether, it was a most unhealthy atmosphere in which to carry on peaceful scientific pursuits.

Still Dr. Bohlin remained on the job. He was continually visited by bands of Chinese soldiers, all of whom were potential brigands. For weeks he was isolated, although only forty miles from Peking. He never could be sure that he would live to see another day. But the young scientist would not give up. For six months he worked at the excavation, which proved to be of much greater magnitude than had at first been anticipated. Fissures in the limestone rock had been filled with sediments and many tons of material were removed. Some great blocks containing bones were taken out intact; much debris was sifted for possible loose teeth. Valuable animal fossils were found, but not a trace of human remains.

On the afternoon of October 16, three days before the work was to be ended for the season, Dr. Bohlin made an important discovery. Embedded in the face of the exposure was another human tooth. It lay close to the spot where the first two teeth had been found. On the way back to Peking he was stopped a dozen times by soldiers. They little knew that he was carrying one of the world's most valuable scientific specimens in his waistcoat pocket. When he reached the city he went straight to Dr. Black. Even his wife did not know that he had returned. At half past six o'clock in the evening he delivered the tooth.

Dr. Black began to study the specimen almost at once. He found that it was the first lower molar of an individual about eight years old, and definitely human in character. He entered upon a most exhaustive study, comparing it point by point with teeth of a Chinese child of the same age, of a chimpanzee, and with three early human types, the Piltdown Man, the Heidelberg Man, and Neanderthal Man; also with two ancient fossil apes believed to be in the ancestral primate stock.

Like myself, Dr. Black worked best at night. Now and then I used to discover him, in the small hours of a Peking morning, out for a breath of air. We might drop in for a bite to eat at an all-night restaurant. Then I'd hear the latest bulletin on the tooth. Black was a splendidly equipped man to do the job. He simply devoured work. His paper on the tooth was completed in record time. It showed pretty clearly that Peking Man warranted the erection of a separate genus of its own, *Sinanthropus,* distinct from the genus *Homo* of modern man. It was a masterly dissertation, and Dr. Black went off on a well-earned vacation to Europe and America. Loaned by the Survey, the tooth accompanied him, carried in an ingenious receptacle in his waistcoat pocket. It was literally chained to him. None of the Crown jewels was ever handled more carefully than was that little brown tooth!

Dr. Black exhibited the tooth to most of the world's fore-most authorities on human evolution. They were impressed. But after all, a tooth is only a tooth, even if it does show to the specialist a good deal more than meets the eye of the uniniti-ated. There is a distinct limit as to what can be deduced from such scanty evidence. Most of the eminent anatomists preferred to wait until more data were available before making any pro-nouncements upon Peking Man.

Dr. Black returned to China in the autumn of 1928. The excavations at Choukoutien were continued by Dr. Bohlin, Dr. Young, and Dr. Pei. They had great success. The most important discovery was the right half of an adult jaw con-taining three molar teeth in position and the sockets of three others preserved; also there were twenty or more teeth from individuals of various ages, and the chin portion of a child's jaw; in addition, several fragments of the parietal bones of the skull of an adult and that of a child.

This wealth of new material made us all realize that almost anything might be expected from that superb deposit. Evi-dently it was not the result of stream action, as was at first supposed, but was an actual dwelling cave. The remains of so many individuals in a single spot could hardly mean anything else. The jaw furnished most important information. It is extraordinarily ape-like and yet the teeth are definitely human. The many teeth confirmed all Dr. Black's conclusions as to the genus *Sinanthropus* and its human character. The frag-ments of skull demonstrated that Peking Man was a relatively large-brained type compared to any ape.

Work at Choukoutien continued throughout the autumn of

1929. Dr. Bohlin had left to go exploring with a division of Dr. Sven Hedin's expedition to Chinese Turkestan. The excavations were in charge of Dr. Pei. Early in December 1929, I was present at a farewell tiffin given for a retiring member of the British Legation. Dr. Black was there. When the last speaker had told the guest of honor for the last time how sorry we were to have him go, and the last glass of port had been drunk, I saw Dave Black signaling to me across the table. A moment later he said:

"Roy, we've got a skull. Pei found it on December 2."

He didn't have to explain what kind of skull. I knew that it could only be that of Peking Man. I bundled him into my car and we drove to the Medical College. Two other non-scientific friends followed in another auto. On the way he told me that a new section of the Choukoutien deposit had been opened. Apparently this was a part of the dwelling cave where the bones were but slightly damaged by the pressure of rock and debris. A rhinoceros skull lay close to the human remains.

In Dr. Black's laboratory I viewed the specimen. There it was, the skull of an individual who had lived half a million years ago, one of the most important discoveries in the whole history of human evolution! He couldn't have been very impressive when he was alive, but dead and fossilized he was awe-inspiring. The base of the cranium was still enclosed in a block of hard travertine, but the remainder was exposed. It is almost perfect except for the face, which is gone. The specimen is that of a young adult, and the sutures are distinct. When I thought of the pitiful fragments of other early primitive human types which scientists had studied for so many weary hours, this superb uncrushed specimen seemed an embarrassment of riches. It would tell so much of what is true about the beginning of those peculiar beings called Men, who dominate the earth today!

While we stood there, in came Père Teilhard de Chardin. Everyone in the scientific world knows this charming Jesuit Father, but perhaps not many beyond those realms. He is a great savant, a brilliant palaeontologist, an indefatigable searcher for the truth of human evolution. It was he who found another tooth of the Piltdown Man a year after the first discovery. At the edge of the Ordos Desert in China he dug up the first implements of the Palaeolithic, or Old Stone Age, known from Asia. Père Teilhard is a valued friend of Black's and mine. With him we rejoiced exceedingly.

Such an event under any circumstances called for a celebration. Scientists, even when concerned with the profound questions of the evolution of the human race, are still human in every sense of the word. Therefore, I gave a party. Ten of us gathered at the Hotel du Nord, on Hatamen Street, to eat pigs' knuckles and sauerkraut and imbibe German draught beer. In that little gathering eight nationalities were represented—Swedish, American, Chinese, Canadian, German, French, Russian, and English. We smoked and drank and talked Peking Man until far into the morning.

It soon became evident that considerable time must be devoted to the proper exploration of this prehistoric gold mine and that only correlated field work in neighboring regions could answer some of the problems raised at Choukoutien. So in the summer of 1929 the Cenozoic Research Laboratory, financed by the Rockefeller Institute, was organized as a special department of the Chinese Geological Survey, to conduct the operations. Père Teilhard and Dr. Young went to Mongolia with me on the Central Asiatic Expedition in 1930 and later Dr. Pei joined us to learn palaeontological technique under Dr. Granger. That year the *Sinanthropus* site was purchased by the Geological Survey of China, with the hope that it would thus be preserved for science.

As more and more priceless material was obtained from the Choukoutien deposit, its fame spread far and wide. Scientists from all over the world made the pilgrimage to Peking as to Mecca. Among them was the distinguished anatomist Professor Elliot Smith of London, and the Abbé Breuil of Paris, one of the most eminent experts on the implements of the Old Stone Age. Thousands of cases filled with blocks of travertine containing teeth, jaws, skull fragments, and other specimens overflowed the Cenozoic Laboratory.

Dr. Black worked all night every night, and much of the day. The result of such concentrated application was inevitable, I suppose. In 1934 he died. It was an irreparable loss, both to science and to his many friends. For a time the investigations ceased. Then in 1935 the Rockefeller Foundation, with the approval of the Chinese Geological Survey, invited Dr. Franz Weidenreich, an eminent German anatomist, to continue Black's research. For some months after the Japanese invaded China, Dr. Weidenreich remained in Peiping. When it became evident in 1941 that conditions were becoming impossible for scientific work, he departed for the American Museum of Natural History in New York City. He was installed in the "Tower Room" where Professor Osborn worked many years of his life. There he continues his study of Peking Man and other problems in human evolution.

Dr. Weidenreich already has published many papers on this subject, some of which are listed in the Bibliography at the end of this book. His monograph entitled *The Skull of Sinanthropus pekinensis* (1943) is a comparative study of Peking Man and other related hominids. I have followed his conclusions very closely in this volume.

Although Dr. Weidenreich has a complete series of casts of Peking Man, the originals, we devoutly hope, are still in China. Efforts were made by the Chinese Government to remove them to a place of safety. It was too late. Almost on the day they were to leave the country, the Japanese attacked Pearl Harbor and the ports were closed. They may have fallen into the hands of the Japanese. No one knows. Their fate may always remain a scientific mystery.

CHAPTER EIGHT

A Cave in the Western Hills

ONE BEAUTIFUL MORNING in the autumn of 1932, I stood at the entrance to the cave of Peking Man, looking across the sun-lit plain. Below me lay the little village of Choukoutien beyond a tiny river. A line of ladened camels plodded slowly along a sunken road toward the grim walls of old Peking, forty miles away. Behind them an oxcart pitched and tossed in a cloud of yellow dust. To the left, the beautiful Western Hills swung in a wide arc where the Pa Ta Chu, the "Eight Great Temples," nestled in pine-filled valleys. Beyond them stretched wave after wave of treeless slopes broken by rocky outcrops and covered by a brown grass mantle like an incredibly old garment mended with patches of gray and yellow.

I leaned against a rock, reveling in the view while musing on what I had seen within the cave. My imagination drifted back to the far dim past, to a day 500,000 years B.C. I could visualize Peking Man standing where I was standing then. Not an impressive figure, for he was only a little over five feet tall. Above heavy eyebrow ridges his forehead sloped back in only a slightly rounded curve; of chin he had almost none.

Newly risen from sleep, he yawned, shook himself, and turned back into the cave. There, beside the banked embers of a fire, crouched his mate; half a dozen children still lay in dark recesses on beds of grass, curled like little animals in sleep.

Peking Man was hungry. He poked the fire, threw on a few bits of wood, and looked about for breakfast. But there was no food; only a handful of hackberry seeds cached in a crevice of the rock. These he gobbled greedily, spitting out the shells as he crunched them between his teeth. Shuffling to the cave door he looked out over the plain below. Meat he could see in plenty. But how to get it? A herd of shaggy bison grazed in a green meadow and a pair of rhinoceros stamped and snorted, rooting in the turf like giant pigs. Just beyond a fringe of trees along the river five deer nibbled the fresh grass. Suddenly with a coughing snarl a yellow form launched itself from a clump of bushes, landing on the flank of a feeding buck. Screaming in terror, the animal kicked and struggled, but the tiger's weight bore him down. Great claws ripped livid gashes along his back and sides; at last his moans ended in a choking gurgle as the huge cat sank its teeth in the pulsing throat.

Fascinated, Peking Man stared down upon the scene. He called excitedly. In a moment his mate and a swarm of children, rubbing the sleep from their eyes, clustered about him at the cave door. Together they saw the drama end. One foot on his kill, the tiger threw up his head, roaring a challenge to the animal world. Then he settled down to eat.

For an hour the little group of humans watched the cat tear at the deer's flanks and lick the warm blood spilling in a red stream from its torn throat. At last, gorged to the limit, the tiger ambled to the river and drank his fill. A clump of bushes concealed him from the watching group. With a sharp command the man leaped from the cave platform and ran up the hillside to the very top. Chattering like monkeys, the children followed. From there they could see the tiger leave the water's edge, walk slowly into the long grass, and settle comfortably beneath an overhanging bank.

Peking Man ran back to the cave. His excited brood picked sharp-edged pieces of quartz from niches in the rockwall where each one had concealed his favorite tools. Then to the hilltop they swarmed again. Half a dozen pairs of eyes watched the sleeping tiger for a long time. They could just see its yellow form, close under the bank, stretched at full length. All was safe. He would sleep the whole day away. Down to the plain ran *Sinanthropus pekinensis*, followed by Mrs. Sinanthropus and all the little Sinanthropops. The tiger had eaten the entire hind quarters of the deer, but a goodly portion remained untouched. With their sharp bits of quartz they fell to work stripping off the skin and hacking out great chunks of meat. The children made a dozen trips to the cave. At last nothing remained except the skin. Peking Man draped it carefully about his shoulders, shrugging into its soft folds as he walked up to his home in the mountainside.

The young Sinanthropops scurried out to gather wood. Over the blazing fire they roasted choice bits of meat, but Peking Man appropriated the legs for himself. Between two rocks he cracked the bones and noisily sucked the marrow. Then came the greatest delicacy of all. A few blows of a sharp stone broke open the deer's skull and he scooped out the brain.

That was his dessert. With stomachs distended like ripe water-melons, the whole family filed down to the river to drink where the sweet water ran over a bed of yellow pebbles. Then, even as their benefactor, the tiger, they lay down to sleep in the dark recesses of that limestone cave in the Western Hills.

Thus my imagination drifted as I stood there gazing into the blue distance where the ancient capital of Kublai Khan slumbered in the autumn sunlight. It all seemed very real to me, for I had just been learning the story that this primitive family and others of their kin left behind them half a million years ago. It was a true tale, some of which was as plain as though it had been written on the rocks and left for us to read; other pages were obscure, offering only fascinating hints for speculation. To the cold eye of science these would be labeled "probably," "uncertain," "perhaps." But every bit of evidence, every stone and scrap of bone gave a message of its own which helped to fill in the missing parts of the jigsaw puzzle of human evolution.

A fascinating page, so dim and yellowed by the passage of time that it is difficult to read, is the use of fire. Where did early man first learn to use it, and how? Only one answer is certain. In the beginning it was with the help of nature. It may have been molten lava flowing from an erupting volcano and running in livid streaks among crevices in the rocks. Perhaps lightning struck a tree in the forest. A conflagration started and swept through the woods, driving before it those animals that could escape by speed. Doubtless hundreds of primitive folk perished in the blaze. But some among them learned that water was a safe refuge from the devouring flames. Into a stream, a lake, or a river, they led their frightened brood. They saw the fire pause and die when it reached the water's edge, or sweep around the margin of their blessed haven. Then, when the fire had passed, leaving black desolation in its wake, they ventured out into the smoking ruins. A delicious smell of roasted flesh met their nostrils. Here was a rhinoceros half baked as it lay in twisted torture; there a wild boar, its hair singed off but a smell of roast pork filling the air; an elephant, the lord of all the animal world, steaming on a bed of glowing coals. So much food was unbelievable. True, its taste was different from raw meat to which they were accustomed, but the taste was good. And so they ate and learned that roasted flesh was a delicious feast. They had seen rain fall from the sky on a blazing forest and the flames sputter and turn to steam. Perhaps one among them, with greater intelligence, realized that fire need not be regarded only as a terror of the Infinite loosed upon a hapless world for destruction and horrible death. By feeding it with dry wood it could be kept alive; water killed it quickly. Thus it could be controlled and made to serve their lives and comfort. By means of a burning stick they transferred fire to the place they called home. There it was nourished with wood and made to cook their food and give them warmth in the days of bitter cold.

That is the way it must have happened long before Peking Man came to live in the Western Hills. But that he and all his tribe did know the use of nature's greatest gift we can read in the thick layer of ashes, the pieces of burned wood and charred bones on the floor of his mountain cave. Just to make doubly sure, the scientists tested the soft dark layer chemically. That proved the presence of free carbon in the blackened fossils and earth. Under, and among, these layers were found banded clays of vivid yellow and red. These were the baked sediments which generation after generation of tribesmen had used as hearths on which to cook their food. Thus the question as to whether or not such a primitive type of human utilized fire in his established home was forever settled.

The prehistoric story told by the debris in that wonderful cave settled other questions which had occupied pages of scientific journals devoted to the evolution of the human race. Did Java Ape-Man have intelligence enough to use stones as tools? It was obvious to Dr. Black and others, even at first, that Peking Man was related to, and approximately in the same stage of development, as that of Java Ape-Man. But because the bones of the latter were found in deposits where they had been carried by rivers of volcanic mud, there was no direct evidence as to his use of artifacts or fire. The cave at Choukoutien gave the answer. From one locality alone two thousand quartz fragments and ten stones of a kind not native to the cave were recovered. These include fine green sandstone, quartzite, green shale, three limonite concretions, and two pieces of flint. Among them are flaked choppers and boulders roughly shaped and edged; scrapers used perhaps for preparing skins; pointed implements, and hammer stones. Very little definite shaping has been attempted on the artifacts. Most of the "preparation" apparently resulted from chipping by use rather than preparatory chipping. The flakes were obtained by crushing the pieces between two boulders or side-flaking of the core. Most authorities agree that the Choukoutien artifacts may be regarded as very early representations of the Old Stone Age culture but not related to the sequence of Western Europe. In addition to the stone tools there also occur throughout the deposit vast numbers of burned and broken bones. Seventy-five show definite traces of human workmanship. These are cut and scratched, and the Abbé Breuil suggests that it is possible to recognize distinct evidences of a systematic adaptation of the bones, antlers, etc. into forcing, scratching, or hammering tools.

Dr. Ralph Chaney, of the Carnegie Institution, and palaeobotanist of the Central Asiatic Expedition, visited Choukoutien to study the food of Peking Man. He says:

"Several significant discoveries have been made in these ash layers. Bits of incompletely burned wood have been identified as similar to plants now living in northern China and in other lands of a somewhat cool and dry climate. Abundant fragments of charred bones indicate that here were cooked choice cuts of horses, bison, rhinoceroses and other game animals which ranged the Western Hills and adjacent plains during the past, and which have no living relatives in North China today.

"These animals, used as food by Peking Man, indicate a plains country, probably with trees confined to the stream borders as in semi-arid regions today. . . .

"About twenty feet above this lowest level of human occupation, and occurring in breccia containing numerous quartz artifacts and bone fragments, there is a layer several inches thick, made up of thousands of fragments of the shells of

seeds. The markings on their surface indicate that they represent the shells of hackberry seeds—small globular bodies,
smaller than peas. . . .

"The modern hackberry (*Celtis*) occurs as a small tree in the
forests both of North America and Asia but is most characteristic as a shrub on semi-arid slopes and stream borders.

"It seems certain that large numbers of hackberry seeds were
carried into the cave and their shells crushed while they were
being eaten. The question arises as to whether early man or
some other animal was responsible for bringing them into the
cave at Choukoutien.

"The fruits of the hackberry are like small cherries, skin and
pith enclosing a shell, within which lies the seed. In the more
arid parts of the United States, these fruits are extensively used
as food by birds and rodents and by the native Indians. Certain
trees and shrubs bearing especially large or sweet fruits are
regularly visited by the Indians of the Southwest. . . .

"The fragmentation of the shells in the cave deposits is interpreted as indicating the probability that they represent the
food refuse—fossil garbage it might be called—of the human
inhabitants of the cave, rather than of its rodent population.

"Here then is the earliest record of the use of plant food by
prehistoric man. In a land so cool and dry that there were few
fruits and nuts, Peking Man may be supposed to have gathered
the hackberries from bushes near his home, and to have
mashed them in preparation for his meals as do the modern
natives of our Southwest. . . . " (1935)

The fossil bones of other animals are badly preserved.
Whole skulls are seldom found and very few skeletons. They

appear to have been fractured either by Peking Man himself or by beasts of prey. The remains of a varied and impressive list of mammals were discovered in the cave. Among them was a species of large wolf, a small dog (dingo), a slender fox, two very large brown bears and a small one, a saber-toothed tiger, a leopard, and other cats together with great numbers of hyenas. There were swamp and river dwellers, such as otter and water buffalo. Animals of the rocks and forested mountains are represented by the sika and a flat-antlered deer, the wild boar and the big-horn sheep. Deer comprise about seventy-five per cent of the animal fossils. Obviously Peking Man liked venison. The mammoth, camel, bison, antelopes, a big horse, and ostrich (*Struthiolithus*) seem rather out of place, but nevertheless their remains occur. Perhaps they were accidental wanderers along the plain, coming from some western steppe behind the hills. Only two monkeys seem to have been present, a macaque, somewhat larger than the form now living in North China, and one baboon. All these point to a Middle Ice Age dating for the fauna contemporary with Peking Man.

The cave at Choukoutien appears to have been first occupied by hyenas, as shown by their skeletal remains and great quantities of petrified droppings (coprolites). When Peking Man, on an apartment-hunting expedition, discovered the cavern, probably it had been temporarily abandoned by the animals. After he and his family set up permanent housekeeping they were able to frighten away other beasts, perhaps by fire. It was a palatial home, at least in size. Part of the cave was 150 feet wide. East and west it extended 525 feet. The ceiling was lost in shadows 150 feet above the floor. For century after

Excavating the Cave of Peking Man. 1937

century, probably thousands of years, the descendants of the original Peking Men continued to occupy the cavern. The accumulation of ashes and debris raised the floor, leaving embedded in the refuse the story of past generations. But one day a part of the roof collapsed. Through the gaping hole, detritus from the ground above washed in; blocks of loosened limestone made that gallery a dangerous place in which to live. Once started, the destruction of the ceiling probably continued rapidly. If the successors of the original Peking Man were in residence at the time, they must have been forced to abandon the home of their ancestors for safer quarters.

So it came about that when the "cave" was discovered by Dr. Andersson in 1921, it was not a cave; it was only a great fissure in the limestone cliff filled in with a hard, brecciated travertine. The bones of the oldest known men of continental Asia, and the works they left behind, lie buried in this consolidated mass. To read their story, and recover what one may, the palaeontologists have had to mine into this accumulated deposit. It is a long, slow process, for every basket full of gravel must be sifted and carefully evaluated before it can be discarded. The work is far from finished. Doubtless in years to come the limits of the cave as now known will be much extended and the story of this incredibly ancient tribe will be more fully told.

Up to the present, the remains of about forty individuals, including males and females, adults and children, have been unearthed. There are one hundred and forty-eight teeth, thirteen jaws, and fragments of fourteen skulls, but only four represent fairly complete crania. Other parts of the skeleton are almost non-existent. Pieces of seven thigh bones (femora), two humeri (upper arm bones), a left wrist bone (semi-lunar), and a section of a left collarbone (clavicle) are the only known skeletal remains. The femora show that Peking Man walked fully erect; that he did not stand with bent knees or with his head projecting unduly forward.

Dr. Weidenreich suggests that the reason for the dearth of skeletal material in the cave was due to the habit, widespread in palaeolithic time, of breaking up the bones to get at the marrow for food; also they may have been crushed and carried off by carnivores, such as hyenas and bears. The more or less complete skulls all have fractured bases and the facial parts are missing. A Neanderthal cranium from Monte Circo (Italy) was opened in exactly the same manner. This, with other evidences, leads him to believe that it was done to extract the brain. A similar condition, as we have noted, existed in the baboon skulls found in the cave with the Southern Ape in South Africa and the skulls of Java's Solo Man. Therefore such a systematic and general damage to the basal part of skulls can only be due to design, not to chance. Dr. Weidenreich has shown that scars on the top of several crania indicate that they were inflicted by ax or knife-like implements while the men were still alive. Although we may not like to think of our revered ancestors as cannibals, nevertheless, the evidence is strong that Peking Man killed and ate his kin. He may even have devoured his children if they displeased him, or his own wife. Anyway, if he didn't eat her when she died, probably some of his friends did. It is doubtful that so much good meat ever was wasted.

Peking Man was definitely on the small side. Dr. Weiden-reich concludes that he stood 5 feet 1½ inches and that Peking Lady was 4 feet 8½ inches tall. These estimates were arrived at by a study of the bones in comparison with modern skeletons of known height. Peking Man had a rather small and only moderately projecting face; somewhat more than in modern humans, but not nearly as much as that of a gorilla or chimpanzee. His nose was much lower, broader, and flatter than ours and about the same width from top to bottom. In this he foreshadowed the living Mongoloids. He did, of course, have "beetling brows." His forehead was much more flattened and receding than ours but somewhat less so than in Java Ape-Man, and showed a nice little swelling for an enlarged frontal lobe of the brain. A primitive character is shown by the fact that his skull sloped *inward* from the base upward, so that its widest part was low down and near the back; in all modern men the slope from the base is *outward* and the head is broadest near the summit. An interesting feature is the bony ridge (mid-sagittal crest) along the top of his head like that found in ancient and modern Chinese, Eskimos, Australians, and American Indians. The skull walls are very thick as in all primitive types. As the brain increases in size, the bony structure becomes thinner to accommodate the expansion. In brain capacity Peking Man averaged 1075 c.c. while his Java relative can boast an average of only 870 c.c. Modern man averages about 1350 c.c.

Regarding his jaw, I can report just about as much progress as we could have expected to see in such a primitive type. Apes have jaws with teeth arranged in a narrow horseshoe arch, while ours are wider across the back and flatter in front. Peking Man resembled the apes in this respect. His teeth are primitive, big, and in some instances larger than the comparable teeth in apes. The molars are all bigger than in modern man but show a tendency to reduction of the third molar. In modern man the third molars (wisdom teeth) are smaller and sometimes fail to erupt. The eyeteeth (canines) although by no means as large as in the gorilla, are bigger and much longer rooted than in modern humans. He did, however, have the shovel-shaped incisors or front teeth, in which some moderns rejoice. Peking Man had one great advantage over us; not one of the one hundred and forty-eight teeth and thirteen lower jaws shows the slightest sign of caries, pyorrhea or other dental troubles. All this without the benefit of advertised tooth pastes!

Dr. Weidenreich's exhaustive study has led him to some startling and profoundly important conclusions. He believes that the Peking and Java Ape Men form a closely related group; that both are in the direct line of modern man's ancestry and that Peking Man shows evidence of relationship to certain modern Mongolian groups. (1943, pp. 276-77) Thus, for the first time our genealogy has been traced back almost to its human inception.

Peking Man and his cave ranks as the most important discovery in the whole history of human evolution. The wealth of skeletal material alone, of this extremely early type, puts it at the top of the list. In addition, it is one of the most ancient and is accompanied by certain data for age determination plus the only known picture of the intellectual status of man in his almost dawn stage. For the first time we know that he used fire, made stone tools, and had a kind of social life. Compared with the few facts one can glean from the fragmentary remains of Java Ape-Man, the cave is an El Dorado.

Enormous credit is due to Dr. J. G. Andersson, the father of Chinese palaeontology, and to the scientific acumen and energy of the late Dr. Davidson Black. Had they not recognized the tremendous implications of those two human teeth discovered by Dr. Zdansky, and obtained the financial support to carry on the investigation, the treasures of Choukoutien might have been lost to science or at best remained undeveloped for many years. Moreover, when one recalls that almost all other finds of primitive humans have been made by accident and much of the evidence destroyed, we can be grateful that the excavation was under such competent direction from the very beginning. The participation of such able scientific men and the masterly conduct of the work is an assurance that little of importance, either in specimens or deductive facts, escaped their vigilance.

Not only was the "Dragon Bone Hill" at Choukoutien the home of Peking Man, but it was also the residence of a peculiar group of modern humans who lived in their own cave on top of the hill in much later times. The discovery known as the "Upper Cave" was made in 1930, but the site was not excavated until two years later. The inhabitants were the earliest representatives of modern man to be found on the continent of Asia. Their description is reserved for Chapter Twelve.

CHAPTER NINE

Piltdown, Rhodesian, and
Heidelberg Men

THE CONTROVERSY that has flared intermittently for half a century over the Java Ape-Man's leg is only a feeble flame compared to the raging fire ignited by the Piltdown Man's jaw. The trouble started when Mr. Charles Dawson found parts of an almost modern human skull associated with a jaw resembling that of a young chimpanzee. Science immediately divided into two camps. Most Americans contended that the jaw did not belong with the skull; that it had been washed into the ancient river bed with other animal bones. The British anatomists were not willing to have their home product dismissed in such a summary manner. They clung tenaciously to the thesis that the skull and jaw were those of a single individual.

Although the argument started very politely, before long it became distinctly heated and less polite. One Britisher and one American hurled broadsides at each other across the Atlantic through the medium of their respective scientific journals. The rest figuratively stood on the sidelines and watched the fireworks. Finally, the contending parties became distinctly personal. They even expressed in print their opinions of the other fellow's brain capacity and implied that it compared unfavorably with that of *Pithencanthropus erectus*. Eventually, however, the majority of both British and American scientists agreed tentatively that Piltdown Man was an early human type combining an almost modern skull with an ape-like jaw. But there were, and are, distinguished dissenters, among whom are Dr. Franz Weidenreich and Dr. Ales Hrdlicka. It is a case where an attempt to reach definite conclusions from inadequate and problematical material has led only to speculation and individual opinion without the possibility of definite deductions. The whole question is a mass of uncertainties, but in spite of that the specimen is so important that it cannot be dismissed without consideration in any account of primitive man. Therefore, here is its story, which has become as much a classic of human evolution as Dubois' discovery of Java Ape-Man.

Mr. Charles Dawson, a lawyer of Lewes, near Brighton, England, is one of those individuals whose avocation became more important than his vocation. In fact it made him famous. He is an amateur archaeologist, and a good one. I can imagine that during the perusal of dry briefs, his mind often wandered to his hobby. Probably he thought how much more interesting it would be to explore the countryside for objects of natural history than to argue a case before a jury. Be that as it may, on one of his days off in 1908, he was walking along a country road, near Piltdown Common, Sussex, when he "noticed that the road had been mended with some peculiar brown flints, not usual in the district." (Strangely enough, this incident was similar to the equally important one in the discovery of Peking Man when Dr. Andersson saw bits of quartz, foreign to the geology of the immediate vicinity, near the site of Choukoutien.) Mr. Dawson was interested in the flints and learned that they came from a gravel bed on a farm "four miles north of the limit where the occurrence of flints overlying the Wealden strata is recorded." He asked the workmen to preserve any fossil bones they might find in the deposit and on a subsequent visit was given a piece of the parietal bone of an unusually thick human skull. Only that single bit which, by luck, had been preserved! It has been reported that the men found nearly the entire skull but thought it was a "petrified cocoanut" and destroyed the cranium, scattering the fragments. Mr. Dawson made periodical visits to the spot but it was not until three years later, in 1911, that his perseverance was rewarded by finding the frontal bone, including the upper corner of the left eye socket of the skull, on a dump heap.

The obvious age of the bones and their unusual thickness seemed to him of importance, so he took them to Sir Arthur Smith-Woodward of the British Museum. I can imagine the quiet but intense interest with which that charming, white-haired palaeontologist received them. He and Dawson decided to hire their own workmen and make a thorough scientific investigation of the deposit and dump piles, after the floods had subsided, for the gravel pit is usually under water five or six months of the year. Parts of the upper skull, of the

ear region, the occiput, and half a lower jaw containing two
molar teeth rewarded their efforts. The two last named lay
in the lowest gravel stratum where the first fragment was
found in 1908. Presumably these were in their original position.

When I visited Piltdown in 1926 with Sir Arthur Smith-
Woodward, I tried to visualize the region as it must have been
in those far dim days when early men roamed the countryside. History records that when Caesar invaded England it
was densely forested. Ages before that, the River Ouse flowed
beneath what is now the Common, transporting the gravel in
which the famous skull was found. Today the forest has disappeared, leaving an open, heather-covered plain. The site itself is an unimpressive spot to be the subject of one of the most
baffling problems of human evolution. In a lane, at the end
of which is Barkham Manor, between the road and the
hedge, I looked down upon a shallow trench some hundred
and twenty-five feet long by a dozen feet in width and not
more than three or four feet deep. The river deposited these
dark brown gravels hundreds of thousands of years ago. Piltdown Man had fallen in the river, or he had died upon the
bank and his body had been caught by the water, perhaps at
flood time, to be carried downstream. No one knows how far
it traveled. Eventually it came to rest in what is now a quiet
country lane, to be covered by layers of lighter sediments. Two
important "ifs" were responsible for its discovery. The skull
might have remained in its natural grave forever and a day,
if the iron-like gravel had not proved of value in the prosaic
work of road mending, and if Charles Dawson had not happened upon the scene at the time he did. Because the matrix,

and everything it contains, has been stained a deep brown by iron oxide, it is well-nigh impossible to distinguish the fossils. Only by the utmost perseverance and careful work on the part of Dawson and Smith-Woodward were the specimens recovered. They sifted and examined every ounce of gravel over many yards. Probably no more difficult conditions for fossil hunting could be devised.

Crude implements (eoliths), some rolled and abraded, and a sixteen-inch piece of mastodon leg bone, pointed at one end and pierced by a hole at the other, appeared in the deposit. It also contained water-worn fragments of horse, beaver, hippopotamus, a primitive elephant (*Stegodon*), and a mastodon. Apparently these are not all of the same geological age. Although the stratified gravel is Pleistocene, some of the animal remains, consisting of worn and broken fragments, appear to have come from an earlier Pliocene deposit. In 1913 Dawson and Smith-Woodward, by a near miracle, found two tiny nasal bones, and Père Teilhard de Chardin discovered an ape-like canine tooth in August of the same year.

The original site appeared to be exhausted, but in 1915 Dawson's attention was drawn to a new spot, two miles away, by the same peculiar flints that first attracted his interest. There, in a plowed field, where piles of stones had been raked together, he found three fragments of a second individual— a bit of the forehead (frontal) near the right eyebrow, the middle part of an occipital bone, and the left first molar tooth. These agree with corresponding pieces of the initial specimen so far as thickness of the bone and mineralization are concerned, although the tooth appears to show that the second man was somewhat younger. This dramatic discovery came as a heaven-sent reinforcement to the British scientists and brought into their camp several distinguished authorities who, until then, had been strong opponents of Piltdown Man with its ape jaw. Professor Henry Fairfield Osborn was among them.

In 1912 Sir Arthur Smith-Woodward had named the original find *Eoanthropus dawsoni,* "Dawson's Dawn Man," and made a restoration of his skull. The job was just about as difficult as could be assigned an anatomist, because none of the fragments touched each other. Smith-Woodward was doubtless influenced by the ape-like jaw and gave his reconstruction a brain capacity of only 1070 c.c. This is very small, for Dubois' original Ape-Man measured up to 914 c.c. Sir Arthur Keith did not like it at all. He made his own reconstruction, enlarging the skull to a brain capacity of 1500 c.c., which is well above the 1350 c.c. average for modern man. These two reconstructions, so different in the fundamentally important matter of brain capacity, left the scientific world aghast. Then it was that Keith's colleagues submitted him to a scientific test. He maintained that he could make a reconstruction of any skull, even with pieces as small as those of the Piltdown cranium.

"Of course you can," said some of his fellow-anatomists, "but how accurate will it be? That is the question."

"Give me four segments, from any skull unknown to me, corresponding exactly to the Piltdown fragments and we'll see how good I am," Keith said in effect.

His colleagues produced four pieces of an Egyptian woman's skull. Just to make it really difficult, the lady's cranium was very peculiar in shape.

"Now," said they, "build her up."

Keith worked only two days on the reconstruction. Then he sent it to his inquisitors. They compared it with the cast of the original skull. Except for a few unimportant errors, Keith had done an amazing job. His estimate of the Egyptian's brain capacity was 1415 cubic centimeters; the original was 1395 c.c.— just 20 c.c. difference! It was a pretty satisfactory test of what an expert, using the methods of modern science, can do.

Subsequently Keith did reduce the brain capacity of his restoration to 1400 c.c. Sir Grafton Elliot-Smith also tried his hand at restoring the skull, as did Columbia University's Professor J. Howard McGregor. Six or seven restorations were eventually made, each one differing from the others in important particulars. Had the fragments definitely touched each other at some point, the whole matter would have been much simplified.

Although the internal surface of several fragments of the skull were the only basis for a brain cast, attempts were made to estimate the man's intelligence. Sir Elliot-Smith, one of the foremost students of the brain, regarded it as "being the most primitive and most simian human brain so far recorded" (1913).

Sir Arthur Keith, on the other hand, took an exactly opposite view. He believed there were no very primitive features of the brain cast and that it was essentially like that of modern humans. Obviously, these could be only personal opinions, for the material is much too fragmentary for anything like certain deductions.

In some respects the human lower jaw is almost as important as the skull in giving information. Apparently the teeth raced far ahead of the jaw architecture in development. We say that a man has a "determined chin" when his symphyseal region is prominent. I hardly think we can safely deduce what was the will power of our primitive relatives from the chins they left us as a legacy. Nevertheless, we know beyond a doubt that as the human race developed, the chin became a really important feature of the face. In a way, it accompanied mental development. The more primitive the man, the less chin did he have. The apes can boast no chin at all. The lower jaw slopes directly backward from the front teeth. Just inside the point of modern man's chin there is a pair of small bony projections to which the main tongue muscles are attached. In apes these projections give way to a depression. The shape of the jaw is of great importance. In modern humans the widest part is at the back in order to give more freedom for the tongue action in speech. In apes, especially males, it is broadest in front across the canine teeth.

Piltdown Man is the most complete human enigma ever presented to the scientific world. Actually there is only one really primitive character about the skull—the thickness of the bones. (Dr. Weidenreich believes even that is not beyond the range of individual variation.) Otherwise, in all essential characters it is that of modern man. But associated with it is an almost completely ape-like jaw. It is difficult to accept such an anomaly even though one is reminded that Nature is full of paradoxes. She certainly has not taken such liberties with any other human type. Yet it is still more difficult to believe that a human skull and an ape's jaw could be found side by side in a Pleistocene stratum, since no other Ice Age apes have ever been discovered in England. The whole problem is a maze of conflictions and uncertainties. I list here a few of the most outstanding.

Uncertainties: 1. The geological age. Pliocene, Pleistocene, or recent? Which? 2. Were the gravel deposits disturbed before the specimens were found? No one can be sure. 3. Was the first skull broken up by workmen and its fragments scattered? Highly probable. 4. The skull structurally is totally unlike what it ought to be if it represents an early Ice Age human. Why? 5. Were the crude flint implements and especially the punctured, sixteen-inch elephant bone, contemporaneous with the human remains? Impossible to tell. 6. The ape-like jaw and its primitive teeth do not conform at all to the skulls. Why not? 7. Is the jaw definitely a part of the skull or was it washed in from somewhere else? *That is the great question.*

Certainties: Here is the other side of the picture. 1. Parts of two individuals were found two miles apart. 2. The jaw, a piece of the skull, the nasal bones, and a canine tooth were found virtually in the same spot and there is no duplication of parts. 3. The jaw and skull bones are fossilized in the same degree and manner. (However, this evidence is not conclusive, as mineralization might take place in the same degree even if the bones were deposited at different periods, given sufficient time for the chemical change.) 4. Although thousands of

Pleistocene fossils have been discovered in England, anthro-
poid-ape remains are conspicuously absent and there is no evidence that they ever lived in England during the Ice Age.
5. The chances that an ape's jaw and a human skull of con-
formable size were washed into the same deposit at the same
time are extremely small.

The problem of Piltdown Man has addled the best scientific brains for thirty-five years. Few authorities have agreed
about much of anything concerning it, particularly not its
evolutionary position or relationship. Dr. Franz Weidenreich,
in his 1943 monograph, throws it out of the line of very primitive types entirely. He believes it is *Homo sapiens,* modern
man, and that the jaw cannot possibly belong to the skull no
matter what were the circumstances of its discovery.

Thousands of pages have been written about the Piltdown
case, each authority attempting, by sometimes extraordinarily
ingenious arguments, to prove the theory to which he has
committed himself. To present even a digest of the pros and
cons in a book of this character would only confuse the reader.
No amount of thought or discussion can produce definite
conclusions. The question never can be settled satisfactorily
until further discovery in England, or elsewhere, either confirms or denies the association of such an ape-like jaw with
an almost modern skull. Piltdown Man should be listed
among the distinguished dead of problematical age and relationship, with the fervent hope that he may be disinterred
for re-examination at some future date under more auspicious
circumstances.

RHODESIAN MAN

Rhodesian Man is another human paradox. He brings to my mind an anecdote related to me by Professor Osborn about the brilliant Professor E. D. Cope. One day Osborn found him in his laboratory regarding a fossil skull with the greatest disgust.

"This confounded beast has completely upset a flawless developmental series," Cope explained. "It doesn't fit anywhere. It just sits there staring me in the face. It ruins my sleep. No one knows about it except me. I've been tempted to throw it out of the window and try to forget it ever existed, but my conscience won't let me."

I am afraid a good many scientists have the same feelings about Rhodesian Man. Even his fossilized skull has been the source of continual anthropological headaches. He is unique, isolated, and problematical. It is difficult to know where to place him or why he existed at all. He cannot be dismissed as an unmitigated nuisance, for there stand his bones, indisputable evidence that this extraordinary human once lived in Africa. His problem is almost as baffling as that of Piltdown Man, although the dilemma is not the same.

But first the story of his discovery. That was accidental, as usual, due to mining operations in a limestone hill, or kopje, of northern Rhodesia; also it was another discovery in a cave. The hill itself is gone—blasted from the face of the earth by dynamite—but at one time it rose some fifty feet above the surrounding level plain. Its sides were pitted with crevices, two great caverns ran deep into the rock, and the summit had eroded away. Thus came its name, "Broken Hill."

One of the caves extended obliquely downward one hundred and fifty feet into the center of the kopje to a depth of seventy feet below the surface of the plain. The shaft, thirty feet wide and sixty feet high, was more or less filled with the fossil bones of bats, rodents, rhinoceroses, zebras, elephants, hippopotamuses, lions, and other typical African animals, together with a few stone implements of Bushman type. A palaeontological paradise! But unfortunately for science, the limestone contained rich veins of vanadium, zinc salts, and lead.

During more than two decades, a mining company had been tearing away the hill with machinery and dynamite, dumping thousands upon thousands of fossil bones into the smelters, because they, too, were impregnated with minerals. No one knows what priceless relics of human ancestry were destroyed. By pure accident, or perhaps some guiding hand of anthropological fate, a Swiss miner, Zwigelaar by name, working with a black boy, discovered the skull surrounded by "bat" bones ten feet beneath a layer of pure lead ore and sixty feet below ground level. That was on June 17, 1921. The skull is almost perfect except for the missing lower jaw. About ten feet away lay an adult male leg bone (tibia) and, at a lower level, a lion's skull.

Zwigelaar examined the cranium with curiosity. Doubtless it was something of a shock to suddenly find a human skull staring him in the face. He may have thought murder had been committed deep in the bowels of the earth not so many years ago. He would be hailed as an amateur detective; his name would appear in the papers! Whatever he thought, Fate whispered that here was a discovery not to be treated lightly. Skull in hand he ascended the shaft to the mining company's office to exhibit his find. The officials were interested. Instructions to the workmen to watch for human remains produced other bones: Part of a pelvis, a left tibia, fragments of a left femur, two pelves, and a sacrum. These were presented to the British Museum in 1921 together with part of an upper jaw and a hip and thigh bone which seemed to belong to another individual—a woman.

No scientist visited the site until 1925, when Dr. Ales Hrdlicka made the long pilgrimage from the Smithsonian Institution in Washington to Broken Hill. With painstaking effort he traced every scrap of information about the discovery, talked with Zwigelaar and other workmen and the mine officials. He learned that the skull and other bones were not found together or at the same time; they came from various parts of the cave and he concluded that the possibility of their association with the skull was remote. Thus the doubt that so often obtrudes itself in the discovery of skulls and skeletal parts of primitive humans appeared again, just as it had in the case of the femur found with the Java Ape-Man; in the Piltdown Man's jaw; and the legs of the Man of the Solo River.

Hrdlicka determined that the main part of the cave had been used for a long time as a dwelling or feasting place of late African Bushmen or Negroes. Many of the larger bones were broken for the marrow, and fractured human remains suggest cannibalism, but there were no human burials. How the Rhodesian skull got into the cavern is a mystery.

Dr. Arthur Smith-Woodward examined the bones sent to the British Museum with the greatest interest. He named it Rhodesian Man, *Homo rhodensiensis.* Then Sir Arthur Keith

Hypothetical Sketch of Rhodesian Man. Note the Heavy Eyebrow Ridges and Ape-like Face

made his own study. In spite of their doubtful association, he concluded that the tibia certainly belongs with the skull, as do the pelvis, thigh bone, and sacrum. They showed nothing especially remarkable. According to his estimates, the man stood about 5 feet 10 inches high, was very powerful and probably weighed some two hundred and eight pounds. He walked erect, neither stooping nor standing with bent knees as did the typical Neanderthalers.

So far so good, but there is a skull to be considered. And what a skull! Nothing like it has been seen before or since. It is that of a beast-man, a fearsome creature who "out gorillas the gorilla." Still the skull is definitely not pathological. Everyone seems to agree to that. It represents a crude variety of man. Massive eyebrow ridges, as large, and even thicker, than those of a male gorilla, form a bar across the forehead. Although vastly more developed than in any other known skull, their character is human rather than ape-like. The cranium is relatively narrow and long but slopes as sharply backward as in some of the apes and with little frontal bulge; the eyes are big and of irregular outline, yet are more human than anthropoid. The face projects forward. The enormous palate resembles what Heidelberg Man supposedly had to fit his known jaw, but the dental arch is more like that of modern man in shape. The teeth themselves are human in character and size, with reduced canines and wisdom teeth. Thus Rhodesian Man presents the disharmony of an almost completely ape face with a more highly developed posterior region of the skull, human-like teeth and palate, and an erect posture. Nature appears to have taken delight in producing an anthropological paradox.

This particular individual must have had a vile temper. Anyone who suffered from toothache, as he did, could be excused for snarling at the world. One tooth from his upper jaw is missing and ten of the other fifteen are badly decayed. Moreover, their roots show abscesses. As if that were not sufficient affliction, two perforations in front of the left ear appear to have been mastoid abscesses; also one of the leg bones exhibits a growth about the joint. If it belongs with the skull it might indicate rheumatism arising from the infected teeth. Dr. Yearsley, who studied the pathological features of the skull, believes that the man died from the septic condition of his mouth. He concludes that the mastoid abscess broke through the cortex at the base of the mastoid and tracked upward into the temporal fossa and eventually down the neck into the thorax, thus causing death.

Rhodesian Man was not so badly off in size of brain, but in development it was pretty primitive. His 1300 c.c. is well within the modern human range. Dr. Tilney says his brain was "human though still in the rough." The frontal lobe shows many ape-like characters, yet was a better instrument than that of any anthropoid. He feels sure Rhodesian Man possessed the power of speech, and "compared with lower mammals he had a more facile association of ideas and could profit more effectively from experience." (1933, pp. 256-57) Nevertheless, with such a low type of brain he could have had but little skill in making or using tools and his language must have been of the simplest kind. Tilney thinks he was far inferior to typical Neanderthal Man.

In estimating the geological age of Rhodesian Man, we confront a blank wall. He might be very old or very young. The associated mammal bones give no help, as the fauna is that which still inhabits Central Africa. There is little reason to suppose it has changed since the Ice Age, for the African continental plateau has long been a stable area. The subtropical climate and environment have remained fixed for many thousands of years. This strange human may have lived in the early part of the Pleistocene and be as old as Java Man, or he may be one of those slowly developing types like the Australian aborigine who persisted in his primitive state until comparatively recent times.

At first glance, of course, Rhodesian Man resembles the Neanderthal type, especially in his massive eyebrow ridges. Most authorities, however, baffled by his confusing jumble of characters, shy off from a definite classification. They prefer to fall back upon the convenient "side branch" of the human stock. Dr. Hrdlicka says: "It is a combination of pre-Neanderthaloid, Neanderthaloid, and recent characters. It is not a Neanderthaler; it represents a different race, a different variety. The specimen does not fit with its surroundings. It does not fit at all with the fine, long, essentially modern Negro-like tibia. It does not fit with any other human remains saved from the cave, skeletal or cultural. It does not fit with anything, the Negro in particular, found thus far in Africa." (1930, *a,* p. 129)

Dr. Weidenreich, however, with the courage of his convictions, places Rhodesian Man as the lowest representative of the widespread Neanderthalian assemblage. This primitive group of Neanderthalians diverge from both the classic and the more advanced Neanderthals. Dr. Weidenreich feels sure that Rhodesian Man is closer to Solo Man, *Homo solensis,* and consequently also to his descendants, the Australians, than to the European Neanderthal forms and their descendants. (1943, p. 250)

A GENTLEMAN
FROM HEIDELBERG

To me, a harassed biographer of primitive man, who has trod uncertainly among the treacherous and slippery rocks in the stream of human development, Heidelberg Man stands as a safe, dry island. I looked forward longingly to the time when I could discuss him in this book. Here is a specimen, at last, about which the savants universally agree. He has caused no bitter disputes; no international quarrels. He occupies a position in human ancestry as solid as the Rock of Gibraltar.

Piltdown Man suffered distressingly from having a strange jaw. It prevented him from obtaining enough votes from the College of Electors to insure an incontestable niche in the Hall of Fame of Human Evolution. But it was a jaw alone that placed Heidelberg Man among the Immortals. Yet he has a decidedly peculiar jaw. If there were no teeth one might well believe it was that of an ape. But the teeth—not one but sixteen—solidly rooted, each in its respective socket and definitely human, have closed the mouths of the most voluble congenital dissenters.

True enough, there is a slight disagreement about his geological age. But whether he was a product of the First or Second Interglacial periods is a mere bagatelle of a few hundred thousand years and does not materially affect the picture. In any case, he is probably the oldest known definitely human fossil and the recognized progenitor of Neanderthal Man.

133

His disinterment was another of the fortuitous happenings so frequent in the history of primitive human discovery—a combination of accident and scientific perseverance. The Neckar River, a tributary of the Rhine, was responsible for laying down a series of sediments consisting of two thick layers of wind-blown loess, and several of stratified sand and clay. Those sediments were useful commercially, so a great sand pit was dug against the side of a valley near the village of Mauer, six miles from famed Heidelberg University, in Germany.

Because the University of Heidelberg was near; because Dr. Otto Schoetensack was Lecturer on Geology at the University; because the sand pit had yielded a copious supply of fossils; because the Herr Doktor firmly believed that primitive human remains eventually would be found among the bones; because he was a man of great perseverance and made almost daily visits to the excavation for twenty years; and because he had infected Herr Rösch, owner of the pit, with his own enthusiasm—because of all these "becauses" the jaw of Heidelberg Man was discovered October 21, 1907.

A workman, digging in an undisturbed part of the pit eighty feet below the surface, unearthed half of the jaw. His shovel had cut it in two but he carefully excavated the remaining part. Even though it had been damaged and the crowns of four teeth broken, the restoration was simple. All the workmen had been warned to watch for fossils, so he immediately informed Herr Rösch, who telegraphed Professor Schoetensack. The professor broke all speed records in reaching Mauer. Once safely back in Heidelberg, he cleaned and repaired the jaw and published its description in 1908. Since then the valuable specimen has been preserved in the Palaeontological Institute of Heidelberg University.

As the remains of a human being, the jaw was utterly alone in the pit. Not a scrap of skull or skeleton or even of stone artifacts kept it company. But an impressive array of fossil animals had shared the lonely burial for almost a million years. There were the Etruscan rhinoceros, elephants, bears, deer, cats, lions, bison, beaver, and two types of horses. With the exception of the Etruscan rhinoceros, it is fauna of the Second Interglacial period, namely, the warm period after the second glacial advance had ended and before the third had begun.

The gentlemen to whom the jaw belonged and the animals must have been contemporaries, so they fix his geological age as close to three-quarters of a million years. Just as if we found the jaw of a man buried with the chassis of an early vintage motor car, we could date him as the end of the "Gay Nineties" or the beginning of the twentieth century. No other human specimen, with the possible exception of the child of the Java Ape-Man's great grandfather from Modjokerto, can claim with any certainty an antiquity so great as the early part of the Ice Age.

If the Piltdown Man and some of his associated animals had lived together and were not washed into the River Ouse from different geological strata, he would be a near contemporary of Heidelberg Man. But the *if* is an insurmountable barrier as his case stands today. Even so, the pair could not possibly claim close relationship, for their respective jaws and teeth are far apart anatomically.

It is most unfortunate, but not so strange, that only the jaw of the Heidelberg Man was found. The current doubtless had broken up the skeleton in its passage down the Neckar River, rolling it over and over against rocks and ledges until the jaw alone remained intact. More reason, too, for its preservation when one examines the jaw. Until the "Giant of Java" was discovered in 1941, it stood as the most massive human mandible known to science. It could have withstood a violent pummeling from tumbling waters without a fracture.

If one looked at the jaw bone itself, and forgot the teeth, one would say it belonged to a powerful ape. It just about matches that of a female orangutan in size. The ascending blade which articulates with the skull is not very massive but is enormously broad. The lower part is thick and heavy and a chin is completely lacking. Instead of having the two projecting spurs for attachment of the tongue muscles, as in modern humans, there is the characteristic ape pit, or depression. Thus the tongue could not be used as freely as we do ours and speech was hampered. Still, he could certainly talk. With all these ape-like characters, the proportions of length and breadth are human. Very important is the arch of the tooth rows. Instead of being widest in front across the canines, as in apes, particularly males, it spreads apart in a perfect horseshoe pattern.

So much for the jaw architecture. Now, a word about the teeth. Not even the most conscientious objector has a leg to stand on in suggesting they are not human in size, form, and arrangement. As a matter of fact, the teeth so much resemble our own that were they not firmly rooted in the ape-like jaw one might well think they were the teeth of a husky modern man. The teeth are somewhat larger than modern teeth, but are rather small for the jaw structure, and the canines do not project above the tooth line. They could not, therefore, have been used for fighting as in large apes like the gorilla. They do have pulp cavities which extend deeper into the great roots than do ours, but this foreshadows the condition in Neanderthal Man.

Even the most courageous anatomist could not make a restoration of Heidelberg Man's skull except by pure guesswork. Because of his relation to Neanderthal Man he probably resembled that race in general character. We might expect a broad, heavy, somewhat projecting face, massive eyebrow ridges and a "bull neck." His food and life must have been that of other primitive men. That, however, is about as far as anyone can go safely.

It is not surprising that no stone implements were associated with the jaw in the Mauer sand pit. Crudely shaped hand axes, such as those found in France, Belgium, and England in deposits of similar age, are the sort of tools he probably used. These are heavy and would not be carried by the stream current to such a distance as the lighter bone.

Heidelberg Man lived in a pleasant country of meadows and forests. Among the trees, the red deer browsed on the leaves and the lion browsed on the red deer. The straight-tusked elephant stalked ponderously along the edge of the meadows where the long-legged, two-horned Etruscan rhinoceros, the bison and aurochs and the Mosbach horse, nibbled the grass. When he heard the roar of a lion on its kill, he watched hungrily from the shelter of the trees until the King of Beasts had eaten his fill and lay down to sleep. Then he stole up cautiously to glean what he could from the still warm carcass.

He lived a comfortable life. A long period of warmth and moisture had followed the retreat of the glaciers and he could roam the forests and meadows at will, sleep where night found him, and bask in the sun like a contented animal. It is a pity that we do not really know something of his life. What I have written about his way of life is only guesswork. That he used stones and sticks for weapons is a reasonable assumption. He may have discovered the use of fire and kept it alive for a time from a forest blaze set by lightning. He doubtless communicated his simple thoughts in some half-language to others of his kind. But he has left nothing behind to tell the story of what manner of man he was, except his jaw. Still, that single jaw announces definitely that he was a man, probably the oldest of any known humans.

Heidelberg Man was a Neanderthal in the making. Apparently he was one of those forms that had made unusually rapid progress from the Forest Ape stage toward human status. An earlier type with teeth like those of Peking Man must have been the ancestor of Heidelberg Man and lived in Europe or west Asia long before the Ice Age.

CHAPTER TEN

Enter the Cave Man

"CAVE MAN STUFF" of modern vernacular is inevitably associated with Neanderthal Man. In the popular conception he is a terrifying, beetle-browed, bull-necked, pot-bellied individual covered with shaggy hair. Armed with a great club, he is shuffling through the door of his cave, dragging a female, presumably his wife, by the hair, she wearing an appropriate expression of horror.

Marcellin Boule, the distinguished French anthropologist, is responsible for the traditional picture of Neanderthal Man's physical appearance, but American cartoonists have supplied the domestic details. Boule's restoration was made in 1913, based upon the "Old Man of La Chapelle." With many of the skeletal parts missing, it is not surprising that he emphasized the gorilloid aspect of the type. But since then more than a hundred skulls and skeletons have been discovered and his anatomy is better known than that of any other primitive human. He was far from being a beauty, but not so ape-like as at first supposed. It will take many years, however, to eradicate the original conception from the public mind.

Even though Neanderthal Man's appearance left much to be desired in the way of pulchritude, and his brain was not of the highest type, nevertheless he was not a fool. He could talk perfectly well and doubtless had a language sufficient for his needs. He could *make* fire; could fashion stones into varied and useful tools; could compete successfully against the world's most fearsome animals such as the hairy mammoth, tiger, cave bear, and woolly rhinoceros; was able to maintain himself throughout the bitter cold of the last glacial period; had learned to bury his dead; and he had developed a social organization and a rudimentary religion. Moreover, he continued to exist and dominate Europe for many thousands of years. No indeed, we need not be ashamed of him even as a direct ancestor.

Neanderthal Man first came to light in August of 1856 under unfavorable circumstances. The world was not "primitive man conscious" at that time, and scientific thought had not advanced to the point where it was willing to accept the fact that humans of a different species from modern man had lived in the remote past.

In the Neander Valley, a limestone precipice rises above the Düssel River not far from the German city of Düsseldorf. Because it is one of the most beautiful spots of the surrounding countryside, it has been used for generations by picnic parties and by schools for holiday excursions. The name is in honor of Joachim Neander, a poet and song writer of the late seventeenth century. He loved to visit the gorge and doubtless often sat in the entrance to the "Felderhoffer Grotte," all unaware that beneath him lay a human skeleton destined to write indelibly his name on the pages of history. How amazed, and probably hurt, he would have been, could he have known that undying fame would come to him, not from the songs he wrote but only because the bones of a primitive man were discovered in the valley that bore his name! Fortunately, or unfortunately, as one may view the case, the surrounding cliffs of Devonian limestone were so valuable that they were rapidly disappearing into the kilns of a commercial company, forever destroying the beauty of the poet's valley.

By 1856, quarrying operations had reached the Felderhoffer Grotte sixty feet above the river's level. The cavern was divided into two parts and opened upon a narrow plateau from which the rocky wall descended perpendicularly to the river. When the workmen dug into the loam on the floor of the smaller cave, they uncovered a human skeleton. To them it was of little interest. Bones were bones. Shovel them out. But they did, by chance, mention the find to the owner of the quarry. He was unhappy at the desecration, as any gentleman ought to be. "Collect the bones," said he, "and bring them to me at once." Fourteen pieces of the skeleton were recovered, including the skull cap. These were put into the hands of Dr. Fulhrott, a physician living in the neighboring town of Elberfeld, who eventually brought them to the attention of Professor D. Shaafhausen, of Bonn. The Herr Professor concluded that the skull represented a form not known to exist "even in the most barbarous races." Moreover, said he, they antedated the Celts and the Germans and in all probability "derived from one of the wild races of northwestern Europe, spoken of by Latin writers and which were encountered as autoclithones by the German immigrants. And third, it was beyond doubt that these human relics were traceable to a period at which the latest animals of the Diluvium still existed; though no proof of this assumption, nor consequently of their so-termed fossil condition, was afforded by the circumstances under which the bones were discovered." (1857)

Dr. Rudolf Virchow, the most distinguished German anatomist of the day, did not agree with Shaafhausen. He was inclined to look upon the skull as pathological—that of an idiot. Others followed his lead. Even the great geologist, Sir Charles Lyell, when he visited the cave in 1860, never suspected that he was looking at the dwelling of an Ice Age man. When Lyell returned to England he showed a cast of the skull to Professor Huxley, who stated it was the most apelike cranium he had ever seen, but finally concluded it represented an aberrant modern man. These adverse opinions from the most distinguished authorities of the day put a quietus on the discussion. But Dr. William King, Professor of Anatomy in Queen's College, Galway, Ireland, would not be hushed, to his everlasting credit. He again brought the matter to the fore in 1864 by describing the specimen as a new type of human, *Homo neanderthalensis*. The bones were preserved in the Provincial Museum at Bonn, where they rest in peace today.

As a matter of fact, this was not the first discovery of Neanderthal Man. A skull had been found accidentally, in 1848, in the Forbes Quarry on the north face of the Rock of Gibraltar during blasting operations for the emplacement of a battery. The dynamite opened a crevice, and there was the skull gazing at the workmen out of its sightless eyes. The terrace where the skull lay was possibly the floor of a cave. Part of it still exists and was explored in 1911 by W. L. H. Duckworth, but without results. The history of this important specimen is clouded in uncertainty. All we know is that it was presented to the Gibraltar Scientific Society by the Secretary, Lieutenant Flint, but for many years received no attention. In 1862 it found its way to London with other material from the Gibraltar caves, and in 1868 reached its present home in the Royal College of Surgeons. Several anatomists studied it at various times, all of whom recognized that it represented a woman of great antiquity and Falconer even proposed it as a distinct variety of human, *Homo colpiens,* after Calfe, the old name of Gibraltar.

It was not until 1886, however, that these two great discoveries came into their own. By that time Darwin had focused the world's attention on the origin of man. When two skeletons were disinterred near Namur, Belgium, in the rock shelter of Spy, together with the remains of mammoth, woolly rhinoceros, horse, stag, reindeer, bison, and cave bear, and flint blades, points, and other implements, the scientific world suddenly realized the importance of the specimens it had had in its hands for more than thirty years. A determined search began throughout Europe for primitive human remains.

The Spy skeletons were preserved in the University of Liége until the German invasion of 1914. At that time M. Lohest, one of the original discoverers, concealed them in the bottom of an old chest in his home. The Germans had marked the historic specimens as scientific loot, but were unable to find them, and they remained safe in the house until at least 1927, when Dr. Ales Hrdlicka examined them for the last time.

Another very important find was made in 1899 at Krapina, near Zagreb, in Yugoslavia. This is one of the few instances where the discovery was the result of prolonged and painstaking exploration by qualified scientists. The remains of more than twenty individuals were recovered. When I visited the site many years later I saw a shallow hollow eroded out of the sandstone by a small stream, the Krapinica, which now flows nearly a hundred feet below the cave level. I was told that a great many stone implements together with the remains of rhinoceros, bear, beaver, cat, otter, horse, pig, and other animals were found associated with the human bones. Most of the latter were fragmentary but represent young, adolescent, and old individuals. The breakage and burning strongly suggests cannibalistic feasts and not burials. After the brains had been removed as tid-bits the skulls were tossed aside.

In 1908 the "Old Man of La Chapelle" was discovered in the Correze district at La Chapelle-aux-Saints by three French priests. They were exploring a small cave in the terraced side of the Sourdoire River and unearthed the skeleton of a Neanderthal man, lying on its back with the arms and legs flexed. The body had been protected by flat stones and surrounded by skillfully worked flint implements of Mousterian type. The cave yielded more than a thousand artifacts as well as bones of the woolly rhinoceros, reindeer, cave hyena, boar, bison, ibex, and horse. The "Old Man's" skull was broken and parts of the skeleton missing, but he became the subject of a masterly study by Professor Marcellin Boule. From this monograph came the traditional picture of Neanderthal Man.

France has given us other beautifully preserved specimens from La Quina, La Ferrassie, and Le Moustier. Remains have been found also in Germany, Belgium, Italy, Spain, Gibraltar, Malta, Palestine, North Africa, the Crimea, and Uzbekistan, Central Asia. Thus we see Neanderthal Man as Eurasian rather than only European in distribution and divided into many local varieties. Strangely enough, no Neanderthal bones have been found in England although the evidence of Mousterian type implements and the accompanying characteristic animals definitely show that he lived there.

The great wealth of material from these widely separated localities include children, young men and women, middle-aged individuals, and those who had approached senility. Thus it is possible to picture the physical characters of the type very accurately. The average height of the men was 5 feet 4 inches and that of the women 4 feet 3 inches. Neanderthal Man had a thick torso, broad, sloping shoulders, a barrel chest, short neck, long arms, short heavy legs slightly bent at the knees, flat feet, and big hands. Atop this unlovely body was an enormous head, pointed or "bun-shaped" behind, depressed above, and with a low, retreating forehead. Massive bony ridges arched over the eyes, his nose was wide, his upper lip long, and his whole face projected. Of chin he had almost none but his jaw was massive and prognathous. With his strong teeth and jaws he could have given a nasty bite, and probably did, although the canines do not project above the tooth line as in apes who use their teeth for fighting. He was a slow-moving, clumsy individual, for his lower leg is much shorter in proportion to the thigh than in any existing race. In all fleet-footed people the shin is long and the femur short. The articulation of the shin bone with the ankle shows that he habitually squatted with his legs folded under him. The big muscular hands were not designed for delicate work. Certain features of his skeleton are reminiscent of his ape ancestry, although he was a far better man than any of his predecessors.

Even before this abundance of skeletal material had been accumulated, Dr. Ales Hrdlicka maintained that Neanderthal Man was greatly maligned so far as his personal appearance was concerned. He conceived him to be considerably less gorilloid than Boule supposed. He pointed out that, as in living races, there was great variation in sex, age, and in individuals from different regions, although the general group characters remained constant. Even the heavy jaw with its receding chin was not much beyond the range of variation in living Eskimos, Australians, and in some other races. Also, that the habitual squatting posture of certain modern natives can induce a bent knee stance. During the many thousands of years that Neanderthal Man lived in Europe and diverse regions it would be strange, indeed, if the physical type did not undergo great variation. It progressed from lower to higher forms under the influence of time, geography, climate, food, and other environmental conditions.

In size of brain, Neanderthal Man compares very favorably with our own men and women. As a matter of fact, his brain was even larger than in many modern humans. A female skull measured 1367 c.c. and one old man could boast 1600 c.c., which is considerably greater than the average of living men. Size, however, does not tell the whole story. It is the *development* of the brain that counts. Dr. Tilney does not think highly of Neanderthal Man's brain power because the simplicity of the convolutions and small frontal lobe indicate little advance in the higher faculties. He says: "This apparent failure of the frontal lobe to attain greater proportions must have had far reaching influences upon the life and destiny of these primitive Europeans." (1933, p. 255) By that he surmises that if the Neanderthals had had better brains they would not have been exterminated or absorbed by the succeeding race of more advanced Cro-Magnons. Nevertheless, his intelligence was far above such early humans as the Java or Peking men and not much below some living primitive tribes.

Whether Neanderthal Man was a blond or brunet or boasted more body hair than modern man is a matter of pure guesswork. No one knows when, or why, man lost his body hair. Artists have depicted him as excessively hairy, but this is only because they think that such a gorilla-like creature as he was at first supposed to be ought to have a coat like a great ape. Since he lived during the worst of the last glacial period it is reasonable to suppose that nature helped keep him warm with more hair than we have now. On the other hand, the naked human body can endure a surprising degree of cold when it has been gradually acclimated. The Indians of Patagonia live where bitter gales sweep up from the Antarctic ice cap and yet they use only a single animal skin for covering. Doubtless the amount of hair always will remain a matter of speculation, since it is improbable that a body of Neanderthal Man preserved in cold storage like the Berezovka Mammoth, or chemically, as was the pre-Inca Copper Lady now in the American Museum of Natural History, ever will be discovered.

Almost certainly the Neanderthal Man used skins for clothing. Food and warmth are fundamental needs and his human intelligence would never let an animal skin lie unused. Probably he draped it about his shoulders like a shawl or robe. If he covered his loins it was because his loins were cold. Modesty was not a motive. That instinct arose late in human history and then only as a result of teaching.

Neanderthal Man was an inventor. He made a discovery which revolutionized the entire stone-tool industry and improved the lives of countless generations to come. His predecessors simply selected a natural, roughly shaped stone, and then by repeated blows of another stone improved it by chipping one end to a point. "First axes" they are called in archaeological parlance. The flakes were thrown away as useless. But some Neanderthal carpenter conceived the idea of using the flakes themselves. Probably by accident, he found large flakes could be obtained by a blow or by pressing along the cleavage area of a rock with a blunt stone, an antler, or a piece of bone. Then the flake could be trimmed and retouched along the edge by pushing off minute chips. Behold, he had discovered "pressure flaking" and made himself a whole new kit of tools! There were no patent laws in his time, so he gave the invention to his world, for nothing. We can conceive of him instructing other artisans in his basic discovery, artisans perhaps more skillful than he, who improved upon his technique once he showed them the way. So it developed, after thousands of years had piled upon other thousands, into the superb work of the Solutrean people, who made stone knives as delicate and almost as sharp as a modern razor.

Dr. Raymond Murray has said: "When we consider the superiority of these new instruments it is easy to see why the invention of pressure chipping has been compared to the invention of the crucible in the processing of iron." (1943, p. 145) Central Park in New York City is the favorite repository for memorials. There is even a full-size statue of a dog. Why should the archaeologists not erect a statue to the primitive man who first invented pressure flaking? It would have more import than some that commemorate less important deeds!

The Neanderthals trimmed only one surface of the flake; the other side was left untouched. A roughly triangular tool called the "point" is most characteristic of their culture. It foreshadows the spear and arrowhead of later times. Possibly it was mounted in a wood shaft but of this we cannot be certain. They made, too, a great variety of other implements for hacking, chopping, scraping, boring, drilling, cutting, and sawing. The scraper alone has half a dozen varieties, the usual form being crescent-shaped with an outer curved edge. Another has incurved borders for smoothing wood or bone shafts. Perhaps the newly discovered flakes were most important as skinning instruments and knives, for the Neanderthals lived by hunting.

Pressure chipping sounds difficult but actually it is not. I tried it myself under the direction of one of the archaeologists of the Central Asiatic Expedition, and was amazed how easy it became after I had learned the basic technique. More surprising is the great number of flakes one will push off in fashioning a single tool—as many as two or three hundred!

Probably Neanderthal Man and his predecessors utilized materials other than stone. Bone, antlers, hides, plant fibers, and sinews would naturally figure in their home life, but none have been preserved. Stone artifacts alone survived the passing of hundreds of centuries. Wood, of course, must have been used by all primitive men. The Neanderthals undoubtedly made clubs, wooden spears, and perhaps throwing sticks. A simple shaft of wood, pointed at the end, became the first spear. Very probably they learned to attach a piece of flint to the end with sinews of tough fibers. It is difficult to see how some Mousterian implements could have been effectively used unless they were fastened to a shaft of some kind.

"Mousterian" is the technical name given to the culture of Neanderthal Man. Curiously enough it was discovered and named by G. de Mortellet, in 1869, from the original locality of Le Moustier, Department of Dordogne, France, before the people who made the artifacts were generally known. Many years later, in 1908, a skeleton of Neanderthal Man was disinterred at Le Moustier. It was that of a boy, about sixteen years old. He lay on his side, at full length with the right hand under his head and the left hand extended along his body. Beside him were seventy-four worked flint implements and fragments of animal bones. Since the culture is invariably associated with his remains, and Mousterian type artifacts have been found in many parts of the world where no human bones have yet been discovered, it is inferred that Neanderthal Man had a very wide distribution. Père Teilhard de

Chardin found them in the Ordos Desert and N. C. Nelson, of the Central Asiatic Expedition, discovered artifacts of this type in the Gobi. Nevertheless, "we cannot be certain that all Mousterian type implements were made by Neanderthal Man although we do know that all Neanderthals made Mousterian type implements." It is possible that in Asia, or some other region, a different species of primitive human had invented pressure flaking independently at about the same time it was developed by the Neanderthals. The Mousterian culture was a direct outgrowth of the preceding Acheulian culture, with the abandonment of certain implements and the improvement of others.

CHAPTER ELEVEN

The Picture of a Thousand Centuries

NEANDERTHAL MAN was the dominant, and probably the only, type of primitive human in Western Europe during a very long period—from hundreds of thousands to twenty-five or thirty thousand years. His forerunner, Heidelberg Man, lived during the First or Second Interglacial period, three-quarters of a million years ago. Typical Neanderthals were there during the Third Interglacial period and up to the maximum of the last advance of the ice. On the basis of Heidelberg Man and stone artifacts, Osborn gives them a nomadic plains life of six hundred thousand years. In any event, the race did a pretty good job at survival. I wonder if modern man can do as well!

At first Neanderthal Man enjoyed the temperate, or warm, climate of the Third Interglacial period. Crocodiles sunned themselves on mud-flats and hippopotamuses wallowed in the rivers; straight-tusked elephants roamed the forests and Merck's rhinoceroses grazed on the savanna-like meadows

with bison, wild horses, and cattle. For generation after generation, Neanderthal Man was a happy nomad. Game was plentiful; the weather pleasant. Comfort and easy living became the
order of his day. But thousands of years succeeded other thousands and the climate changed. The transition was incredibly
slow, yet the summers were not as warm as they had once
been. The meadows gradually became treeless plains, and in
the river valleys and on sheltered hillsides, spruce, fir, and
Arctic willow trees appeared. A few reindeer wandered down
from the north, found the country to their liking and stayed.
The elephants left the forest; no longer did hippopotamuses
swim the rivers; wild horses, too, either died or moved away
to warmer climes.

Year by year the cold increased. The summers were short
with floods of rain; snow remained longer and at last hardly
melted at all, consolidating into great ice sheets hundreds of
feet thick. Glaciers formed in the mountain valleys and the ice
moved down relentlessly as far south as Spain and northern
Italy. The Fourth Glacial period had arrived to envelop the
land in ice and snow, clouds and chilling mists. The cold was
bitter. Only Arctic mammals and birds could survive. The
musk ox, today the most northerly of hoofed animals, moved
in with the ice; also lumbering mammoths, woolly rhinoceroses, cave lions, cave bears, and cave hyenas. Reindeer were
there in countless thousands.

Individually, Neanderthal Man had not been aware that a
glacial period was approaching. He only knew it was no longer
comfortable to live continually as a nomad. So he sought shelter under overhanging cliffs, in grottoes and entrances to

caverns. Sometimes his descendants occupied the same home for many generations. Life in the open had ended. He became a cave dweller and remained so until his race ceased to be.

No one really knows what caused the Ice Age. Half a dozen theories have been advanced but none is completely satisfactory. Perhaps the best is that of fluctuations in solar radiation, for the sun appears to give out less heat at certain times than at others. In any event, the result was a lowering of the temperature in many parts of the world.

It is possible that we may have another Ice Age. Meteorologists believe that a drop in the average yearly temperature of only seven to nine degrees Fahrenheit, under present atmospheric conditions, would bring the ice down again. *Greenland and the Antarctic continent are both in the midst of a glacial period today*. They were not always covered with an ice cap. We may well be living in an interglacial stage right now. We wouldn't know. The span of man's life (and particularly recorded knowledge) is so infinitesimally short, compared to geological time of hundreds of thousands and millions of years, that there is no reason to think the ice may not form again over parts of the earth. It is comforting to realize, however, that if the world is afflicted with another glacial advance, the change will take place so gradually, and over so many thousands of years, that no single generation will know what is happening. Even so, if Neanderthal Man could exist in his cave with only skins for clothing while the world was half-covered with ice, our remote descendants will find some means of living in comfort and luxury. Perhaps they will even devise a method for controlling the major forces of nature.

There is nothing very complex about the formation of glaciers. It is merely a question of the amount of snow that falls as against the rate at which it melts. If during the winter there is heavy snow which lies in drifts, and the summer is either too cool or too short to melt it completely, it will pile up into

Mammoths of the River Somme, France

After Mural by Charles R. Knight
COURTESY OF THE AMERICAN MUSEUM OF NATURAL HISTORY

layers and eventually, by pressure, turn to solid ice. If the ground happens to be level, ice sheets will be formed. In the mountains, the valleys will be occupied by rivers of ice which tend always to seek lower levels. Glaciers go down the valleys very slowly as a rule, although in the polar regions they may advance fifty feet a day. Usually the speed is a little greater in summer than in winter and greater by day than by night.

The Ice Age, of course, was not confined to Europe, for glaciers covered a good part of the world. Not Central Asia, however. Professors Berkey and Morris, our geologists of the Central Asiatic Expedition, proved conclusively that the high Central Asian plateau never had been blanketed with ice. Doubtless there was not sufficient precipitation to form glaciers. In Western Europe and parts of America at least three, and probably four, glacial invasions came down from the north, overlaying the land with ice sheets thousands of feet thick, as in the Antarctic and Greenland today. The cold periods continued for thousands of years with still longer interglacial, or warm, stages between each one. The ice retreated for the last time somewhere between fifteen to twenty-five thousand years ago. During the Pleistocene the earth rose and sunk at different places and the sea level changed, possibly because of the enormous weight of the ice. Many land masses, now islands, were connected to larger areas, and animals and humans were enabled to migrate from one continent to another simply by taking a long walk. England and Ireland were joined to the mainland; Europe to Africa at Gibraltar and also by way of Italy, Sicily, and Malta; northeastern Asia and Alaska were connected across the Bering Sea and Aleutian Islands. Over these land bridges the mountain sheep, moose, caribou, and man came to America.

As the ice advanced, cold-loving mammals such as the woolly rhinoceros and mammoth were pushed far south of their original homes. They came down even into France and Spain, there to be hunted by Neanderthal Man. The great beasts sometimes fell into crevasses of the glaciers. In Siberia and Alaska, where the ground still remains permanently frozen even though the ice cap is gone, the bodies of several mammoths have been discovered. The most famous is that of Berezovka. When I was last in Russia, at the Leningrad Museum of Natural History, I heard its story from one of the men who helped prepare the great prehistoric monster of flesh and blood.

Doubtless, he said, it had fallen into a deep snowdrift in a crevasse, for the pelvis and right fore leg were broken. Struggling in the icy pit, it pulled down tons of loose snow and literally put itself into cold storage. There it remained for no one knows how many thousands of years, until the ice cap melted, leaving it embedded in frozen earth. Through weathering, the ground eventually broke away, exposing the head and fore leg. The decaying flesh emitted a horrible odor which attracted the native dogs, thus leading to its discovery. Scientists at St. Petersburg (now Leningrad) were notified and the Czar sent an expedition under the leadership of a Russian zoologist, Dr. Otto Hertz, to collect the priceless specimen. This was in 1901.

My friend told me that the stench of the decaying beast was so awful that Dr. Hertz almost had to abandon the excavation. Unlike any living elephant, the body was covered with woolly, yellowish fur under a thick, outer bristle-like coat which protected it from the cold. Some of the hairs were fourteen inches long and dark rust brown. Thick, stiff hairs formed mane-like patches on the flanks, belly, shoulders, cheeks and chin. Most of the carcass was solidly frozen. The flesh, marbled with fat, was dark red and looked as fresh as beef. None of the men dared eat the meat but the dogs devoured it with no ill effects. The layer of fat beneath the skin was white, odorless, and four inches thick. In the stomach were twenty-seven pounds of undigested food—fir cones and bits of larch, fir, and pine, sedge, wild thyme, several flowers, and two kinds of moss. The frozen blood looked like bits of potassium permanganate; when melted, they turned into dark red spots. The mammoth was skinned, and with the skeleton and much of the internal anatomy, transported on ten sledges nearly two thousand miles over the snow to Irkutsk, on the Trans-Siberian Railroad. In the Leningrad Museum it is mounted in a half-sitting position just as it was discovered.

From the Berezovka mammoth and others frozen in the Siberian ice, we know its externals better than any other prehistoric animal. Its proportions were quite different from the living African or Indian elephants. The head was surmounted with a mass of long hair; a sharp depression marked the neck and a great hump served as a fat reservoir when food was scarce. The hind quarters sloped rapidly downward to the short tail.

The mammoth migrated southward in Europe as far as Rome. As long as it remained close to the ice its invariable companion was the woolly rhinoceros. This animal, too, is well known from a specimen discovered at Starunia in 1911, buried to a depth of thirty feet in asphalt. The remains included the head, left fore leg, and the skin of the left side of the body. It was related to the living white rhinoceros group of Africa and had the same enormous front horn and shorter rear horn on a long narrow head. We know that like the mammoth it was covered with thick wool and long brown hair, had a small fatty hump and a truncated upper lip, adapted to grazing on the grass and herbs it could find under the snow.

Neanderthal Man was always a hunter. He lived primarily on meat. To kill either mammoth or woolly rhinoceros even with a modern high-power rifle would not be without danger. The skins were very thick and the wool and long hair made

Woolly Rhinoceros

After Painting by Charles R. Knight
COURTESY OF THE AMERICAN MUSEUM OF NATURAL HISTORY

them as impervious to darts or spears as steel armor. From the evidence at the great camp in Moravia, the Mammoth Hunters of Predmost, of later Aurignacian Man, it is obvious that primitive man took them by pitfalls. The African natives trap elephants by digging a deep pit in a game trail, placing sharpened stakes upright in the bottom, and covering the light roof with grass or leaves. Once a mammoth or woolly rhinoceros had fallen into such a pit Neanderthal Man could kill it by hurling great rocks on its head and back. Artists depict the primitive hunters as driving mammoths over a cliff. Perhaps they did, but it would not be easy to take either African or Indian elephants that way. The animals are too intelligent.

The Neanderthals must always have had to dispute the possession of their caves with bears, lions, and hyenas. They desired warmth and shelter as much as did man himself. Although his weapons were fantastically inadequate for waging war against such beasts, he had the advantage of fire. That he was successful in his battles is shown by the fact that in the cave of Erhenz-la-Moline, more than eight hundred skeletons of cave bear have been found. The cave lion of France was as big as that now living in Africa and Asia. Both it and the hyena grew thick undercoats of wool and long outer hair to protect them from the bitter cold of the Fourth Glacial period. We know their externals from the drawings of Upper Palaeolithic artists; also, that they survived in Western Europe to the close of the Ice Age. One cave in Sicily yielded two thousand hippopotamus bones; another a thick layer of horse remains; and Keith says that bones of gazelle and fallow deer were abundant in the Skhūl and Tabūn caves of Palestine. Just how these animals were killed with the primitive weapons is a mystery, since the bow and arrow were unknown. It must have required a good deal of intelligence and ingenuity to capture such fleet-footed and timid beasts as deer, horses, and gazelle. I suspect that pitfalls dug about the water holes and on trails leading to their favorite drinking places was the most effective method. Probably his group organized drives for gazelle and wild horses, surrounding the animals and stampeding them over a cliff or through a narrow defile where men waited armed with wooden spears, clubs, and stones. Our Indians used that method and I have seen the Mongols slaughter hundreds of gazelle in like manner.

Neanderthal Man we are certain knew how to make fire, perhaps the most important step in an embryonic civilization. I have related in Chapter VIII how man probably first discovered the use of fire from lightning and volcanoes. But to make it himself was a far different matter. When chipping stones for tools he must have seen sparks fly off; probably he had associated them with fire made by natural causes and realized they could be captured in dry leaves. Thus, he learned what was to change the whole aspect of his life! With the control of fire he could drive out, and keep out, the fierce beasts that disputed the shelter of his cave; could cook his food at will; could warm himself where and when he chose. Without the ability to make fire he never could have survived the terrible cold and dampness of the glacial period. Possibly, and even probably, other primitive men, ages earlier, had learned to make fire. We do not know. But with the advent of the Neanderthals it was a *fait accompli*. Strangely enough, certain primitive living tribes, notably the Andamanese, are not able to make fire today. Thus we see how uneven has been the advance of man's development.

Obtaining and keeping a cave home was not so simple as it sounds. Neanderthal woman could not walk down a valley and see "Apartment to Let" signs inviting her to ring for the superintendent and inspect the rooms. When Neanderthal husband came home tired and hungry from his daily hunting, her problem was not merely to persuade him to accompany her to see the cave of her choice, telling him it was dry and airy, was a good address, and near the favorite range of the mammoth and woolly rhinoceros; that he could sleep late in the morning, get the family meat and be home again to enjoy his marrow and brains before the fire long before dark; that all he had to do was to wait until October first when the present occupants, Mr. and Mrs. Cave Bear, would move to other quarters. Oh no, it was not as simple as all that.

Mrs. Neanderthal may have discovered the cave and had her heart set on moving in. But the chances were that Mrs. Cave Bear was just as determined not to be dispossessed. She and Mr. Cave Bear had enjoyed the comforts of the cavern for many years; they were perfectly happy and did not intend to move on October first, or any other date, for a mere human. Very possibly Mr. Neanderthal was as completely sold on the advantages of the cave as was his wife. But how to obtain possession? A consultation was in order.

With others of his friends he proceeded to arm himself with spears and sharp rocks but, most of all, with fire. By building a smudge at the entrance of the cavern when the wind was right, the Cave Bear family were forced to evacuate or be smothered. Emerging coughing and half-blinded by smoke, the Neanderthal clan had them at a disadvantage. They attacked furiously with wooden spears and sharp rocks. Bleeding and sore, the bears lumbered off, vowing to return.

But Mr. and Mrs. Neanderthal and their little Neanderthals prepared for that. They took possession immediately with all their skins and worldly goods. Across the entrance Mr. Neanderthal and the children built a rampart of stones while the

Little Woman was busy arranging the new apartment. Doubtless the cave bears and cave hyenas returned night after night. Or perhaps a lion coughed his challenge before the entrance. However, possession was ten points of the law to the Neanderthal. Armed with a firebrand, he drove off the wild beasts and made his tenure permanent.

Still, caves were not all one could desire in the way of dwellings. Comfortable enough in the dry seasons, but when the rains came, water often seeped through the limestone roof to run down the walls. The recesses of the cavern were well-nigh uninhabitable. Thus, Neanderthal life centered about the entrance, as shown by the old fireplaces and domestic debris. But the cave did give them shelter and safety from the ever-prowling animals. On fair days the family would gather on the outer platform. We can visualize a Neanderthal group sitting about a blazing fire. The women are dressing skins with stone scrapers, cracking bones of horse, wild ox, and reindeer to obtain the marrow, preparatory to cooking a meal. One of the men, who is clever with his hands, squats with pieces of flint between his legs, pushing off flakes and chipping sharp edges to form a knife. Others scan the valley and plains for game. They know full well what animals can be attacked in the open with spears and the throwing stones found in such great numbers in their caverns. Perhaps they have learned that by placing the missile in a sling they can hurl it far and hard.

When Neanderthal Man moved into caves and rock shelters it was an event of paramount importance. Doubtless it profoundly influenced his psychology as well as his material life. It gave him a feeling of property possession. In the confinement of a cave, beset by blizzards and biting cold, by the most powerful animals the world has ever known, by perils on every side, a feeling of greater dependence upon each other must have knit the family into closer ties. We infer that the first instincts of reliance upon a Superior Being, and belief in a life after death, began to take root in his mind. Whether it was religion, magic, or superstition, who can tell? They are all so closely intermingled that where religion begins and superstition ends is impossible to decide. That is true even today among some highly civilized people of the Orient.

In one Neanderthal cave a row of bear skulls was found which possibly served as a shrine. The dead were interred in front of the rock shelter or at the entrance to the cave with implements to assist them in the other world. At Le Moustier, France, the skeleton of a young man was discovered with the head resting on a pillow of flint. About him seventy-four beautifully worked stone implements were arranged and a hand-ax lay at his left side. Slabs of stone protected the head and shoulders.

The richest treasures were buried with the dead, probably in order to keep its ghost from returning to annoy the living members of the family. This is the underlying reason for similar practices in some existing primitive tribes. The Neanderthals often doubled up the body and tied the knees close under the chin. After all, the dead could not walk if their legs were bound! Thus, for the first time, so far as we know, a primitive people evidence respect for their dead. Instead of eating them, they buried them. Not only does it show a great step forward in human development but it was a boon to anthropologists. Before this time they had had to depend upon the chance preservation of human remains, to puzzle over badly broken skulls and fragments of bones. Now whole skeletons were provided for their edification. As an example, in 1931-32 two caves were discovered in the western slope of Mount Carmel, fifteen miles from Haifa, Palestine. One of them, el-Tabūn (the Oven), was a huge, rather open, cave. It was filled to the top with sediments which to a depth of more than fifty feet yielded a wealth of specimens and showed that occupation had been continuous over a long period of time. The other, el-Skhul (Cave of the Kids), was a grotto with an extensive terrace. Sir Arthur Keith says that evidently the cavern itself played only a small part in the life of the inhabitants, but on the terrace were found ten individuals, men, women, and children, five of whom had suffered no important disturbance since the time of the interment. (1937, p. 42)

Neanderthal Man, like his predecessors, suffered from diseases. It seems to be a general idea that primitive people, living a completely natural existence, remain in perfect health. Nothing could be more erroneous. Animals that have no contact with civilization are sometimes completely wiped out by diseases. So with humans. Neanderthal Man's bones show that he often had rheumatism, pyorrhea, and other infections. There were no doctors, or even "medicine men," in those days. Only the fit survived. Such a relentless weeding out of the weak kept the race as a whole at a high level of endurance. The same is true of the living Mongols. I have seen stark-naked children playing outside the *yurt* when the temperature was below freezing and I was muffled in a fur coat. The lama "doctors" use the most primitive medicines. Except for a few effective herbs their treatment is mostly superstition. Unless nature can effect a cure, the patient dies. As a result, I believe the present Mongols, when it comes to endurance, are equal to the great conquerors of Genghis Khan's time.

Until less than a decade ago it was the almost universal opinion that Neanderthal Man disappeared completely and suddenly from the European stage after the maximum of the Fourth Glacial period, about twenty-five thousand years ago; that his place was usurped by another, more advanced, race of cave dwellers, the Cro-Magnons, true representatives of modern man, *Homo sapiens,* who materialized, seemingly out of thin air. Neanderthal Man was supposed to have died or been exterminated by the invaders, not to have interbred with them, and to have no place in our own direct ancestry. Dr. Ales Hrdlicka, however, vigorously dissented from this opinion and maintained that the Neanderthals were in the line of our progenitors. He remarked that a sudden extermination of the Neanderthals implies an invasion of Europe by a superior race at the very height of the glacial period. This is against the laws of nature which have always directed human movements toward regions of better food and climatic conditions; toward a "place in the sun" and away from the cold. Moreover, such a view postulates a large number of invaders coming from a still greater mother population somewhere in western Asia or northern Africa, and there is no trace of such a colony. Hrdlicka also believed that in palaeolithic times, when man was dependent wholly upon daily hunting for food and without knowledge of the bow and arrow, "logistics" would have made such an armed invasion by a large force impossible. A gradual peaceful extension, on the other hand, would not lead to the extermination or expulsion of the native stock but rather an amalgamation with it. Furthermore, a suddenly invading race would bring its own culture, which would be sharply delineated from that of the resident people. No such abrupt change exists in archaeological remains. Instead, the Mousterian culture of the Neanderthals shows a gradual transition into that of Aurignacian Man.

Moreover, Hrdlicka did not believe that, because the Neanderthals left no drawings and sculptures in their caves, they were necessarily completely devoid of art sense. Many of their implements were beautifully made. He quotes Sir Arthur Evans, who says that "when we turn to the most striking features of this whole cultural phase, the primeval arts of sculpture, engraving and painting, we see a gradual upgrowth and unbroken tradition. From mere outline figures and simple two-legged profiles of animals, we are led, step by step, to the full freedom of the Magdalenian artists."

Considering the anatomy, Hrdlicka could see no valid reason why Neanderthal Man should not have developed into true *Homo sapiens* who immediately followed him. "It is conceivable, if not inevitable, that toward the height of the glacial invasion, the population decreased in numbers, and that the most fit or able-to-cope-with-the-conditions group or groups, eventually alone survived, to carry on. Here seems to be a relatively simple natural explanation of Neanderthal Man, and such evolutions would inevitably carry his most advanced forms to those of primitive Aurignacian and *H. sapiens*—such

H. sapiens as may to this day be seen in the Australian." (1930 *a*, p. 347)

Recent discoveries, particularly those of the Tabūn and Skhūl caves at Mt. Carmel, have tended to confirm Hrdlicka's opinion. Sir Arthur Keith and Theodore McCown see the Skhūl people as most closely related to the Cro-Magnons and intermediate between the Neanderthal and modern man. They believe they cannot be excluded from our direct ancestry. Certainly it would be extraordinary if there was no inter-breeding between the invaders and the invaded. Such is not human nature. Neanderthal Man probably was in part absorbed and in part exterminated by the Cro-Magnons. It is also possible that they may have survived longer in other regions than they did in Europe, for we have seen that they also inhabited parts of Asia and Africa. Nevertheless, their disappearance as the dominant race some twenty-five or thirty thousand years ago appears to have been abrupt and startling.

The problem of Neanderthal Man's position relative to modern man, as well as that of other earlier types, is confusing because the known specimens do not show a gradual transformation of characters from the lowest to the highest type according to geological age and theoretical expectations. This is extremely annoying to a scientist who necessarily has an orderly mind and demands that a species show some consideration for natural laws. They do not always remember that the number of known human specimens is pitifully small; also that exploration for human remains in Asia and Africa is in its infancy and future discovery may clarify the picture. Nevertheless, Dr. Franz Weidenreich has attempted a classification of the Neanderthal group based on structural grounds, after a long study of the available material. (1943, pp. 243-50)

He considers the various types of primitive humans which stand between the Java-Peking men group on the one hand, and modern man on the other, as being sufficiently homogeneous to warrant inclusion in a single large assemblage. For it he uses the term "Neanderthalians." This can be separated into four lesser divisions. Of these, Rhodesian Man stands at the bottom as most primitive, and the Skhūl people at the top as most advanced. The general pattern of the Neanderthalians, he believes, fits perfectly into the broad plan of an evolutionary series beginning with the Java-Peking men group and ending with modern man. He says:

"(1) We now have evidence of the direct transformation of the Neanderthaloid forms into *Homo sapiens;*

(2) The Neanderthalians need not be considered as having become extinct without having left any descendants behind;

(3) Racial or regional differentiations are recognizable within the Neanderthalians themselves and can be traced from there to the races of modern mankind." (1943, p. 250)

Thus Dr. Weidenreich believes we have Neanderthal blood in our veins. Personally, I am not a bit unhappy, for in spite of the original false impression, I have come to admire him and his achievements enormously. Any man who could persist for several hundred thousand years, live through the glacial period, and kill mammoths, woolly rhinoceroses, cave lions, and bears with only bits of sharpened stones for weapons, has my profound respect. I am delighted to acknowledge him as an ancestor.

CHAPTER TWELVE

The Wise Man Appears

A "MYSTERY PEOPLE," tall, blond, and handsome, suddenly sweeping into Western Europe from some Asiatic or African Shangri-La, was supposed to have been the dramatic entrance of modern man upon the world's stage. They were thought to have exterminated the lowly Neanderthals, set up housekeeping de luxe in their caves, and proceeded to decorate the walls with paintings and sculpture. Cro-Magnon was the name given the conquering heroes. Altogether it was a most satisfying picture; just the brilliant way we would have liked our known progenitors to arrive.

But unfortunately most of it isn't true, although until a few years ago it was accepted fact. The Cro-Magnons were men of our own species. Their skeletons testify to that. But other true *Homo sapiens* may have lived in Europe long before their arrival, even as far back as the early Ice Age. I hedge with "may have," because the discoveries of various ancient human skulls in England, Africa, and Europe are thickly clouded in doubt. The geological age or other uncertainties prevent reasonably accurate deductions in every case. Not a single one is satisfactory. So we can only say that the present tendency is to regard true *Homo sapiens* as probably having lived in Europe and elsewhere much earlier than post-Neanderthal time; that he was a contemporary of other less advanced forms.

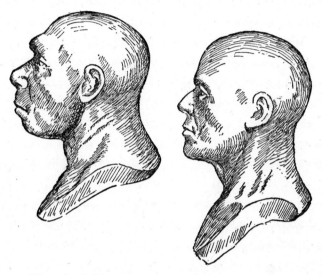

Neanderthal Man (left) and Cro-Magnon Man

After Restorations by Dr. J. H. McGregor
COURTESY OF DR. McGREGOR

Cro-Magnon man has been used as an all-inclusive name, but apparently the typical group was not a "race" separate from other *Homo sapiens*. He was only one representative of the type of modern man in Europe at the end of the last glacial period. Probably the type varied enormously due to different geographical environments, for people in the same cultural stage inhabited Asia, Africa, and perhaps America at the same time. As final blows to the satisfying traditional picture of modern man's appearance on the world's stage, I have to report that our handsome ancestors almost certainly took unto themselves as wives some of the Neanderthal women, unattractive as they were, for skeletons have been found that show a mixture of characters. Moreover, Cro-Magnon men almost certainly did not arrive in Europe suddenly like modern conquerors. The invasion was slow, season by season, extending over many thousands of years. Probably it came as the result of the retreating glaciers and the drying up of North Africa.

But whether or not Cro-Magnon was the first modern man in Europe, he is the first whom we really know. More than a hundred skeletons have been found. His inspiring story is plain for all to read; his civilization is the foundation upon which man has been building ever since. He had heat, light, clothing, and the best technique in stone work the world has ever seen. Religion, magic, and superstition were part of his daily life; with him the fine arts of drawing, painting, modeling, and sculpture reached an amazing perfection. Apparently the use of rouge began with the Cro-Magnon women; doubtless their "hair-dos" were just as important to them as to our own wives and sisters. They may even have had a beauty parlor in some well-lighted cave. Perhaps an especially adept Cro-Magnon lady set up shop for hair arrangements and "facials." She would have been paid in beads, pendants, amulets, ivory buttons, and needles. If the customer's bill had run to large proportions she might have demanded a necklace of fish bones or fox teeth. All these ornaments have been found in their home sites. So many other forerunners of modern civilization figured in their lives that a primitive beauty parlor need not stretch our imagination too far.

The Cro-Magnons were essentially like ourselves. They had high-domed foreheads, bigger brains on the average than ours, for they were bigger men, wide, low eyes, and high-bridged noses; deep jaws with prominent chins. Their heads were "disharmonic" because of the long narrow crania and short broad faces. The men were tall (some more than six feet), broad-shouldered, deep-chested, and the proportions of the leg bones show they moved fast and were very active; quite different from the clumsy, slow-moving Neanderthals. They have been called the finest physical types the world has ever produced. Probably their skins were white. In fact, if you saw a Cro-Magnon man on Fifth Avenue dressed in a sack suit and a Homburg you wouldn't give him a second glance. Or perhaps you might, if you were a woman, for artists depict him ; a debutante's "dream man."

The discovery of Cro-Magnon man was another case of delayed recognition. In the early part of the nineteenth century scientists were not actually burned at the stake for believing that man existed in Europe before the date of the Biblical Adam and Eve, but they did suffer the slings and arrows of outraged public opinion. The contemporary existence of prehistoric animals, however, had come to be accepted as fact. Thus the Paviland cave on the seaward side of the Bristol Channel in Wales became the site of palaeontological investigation. The news that remains of extinct elephants, rhinoceroses, and other animals had been found there brought Dean

Buckland, a geologist of Oxford University, to the scene in 1823. He exhumed the skeleton of a tall individual, stained with red ochre, various fossil bones and ornaments, and implements of bone and ivory from the floor of the cave. The Dean thought he had discovered a Briton lady of the Roman period and that the prehistoric animals had been drowned in the great Biblical flood which swept their bodies into the Paviland cave. Some one named the Dean's find "The Red Lady of Paviland," but, as she was of no more than historical interest, her skeleton rested peacefully in the Oxford Museum for nearly a century. It was not until 1912 that the Abbé Breuil re-examined the bones and recognized the "Red Lady" as a man—the first Cro-Magnon to be discovered.

It was about the time of Dean Buckland's discovery that a Catholic priest, the Rev. J. MacEnery, explored the subterranean chambers of Kent's Cavern on the coast of Devonshire in England. There he found extinct animals similar to those of the Paviland cave together with implements of obvious human workmanship. He concluded that man had lived in England with the mammoth and other Ice Age animals. He said so publicly, but his feeble voice could not penetrate the wall of preconceived public opinion. He did not dare publish his records, which remained in manuscript until many years after his death. Even when ten years later (1833) Professor Schmerling of Liége University found a human skull mingled with fossil animal remains and flint implements in a cave on the banks of the Meuse River in Belgium, prehistorians, including the great geologist Sir Charles Lyell, remained unconvinced of man's antiquity in Europe. But during the next thirty

years changes of vast importance took place in scientific thinking and stirring events happened on the stage of prehistoric
discovery.

In 1852 a miniature landslide exposed the mouth of a small
cave near the village of Aurignac in the south of France. The
entrance had been blocked with a great stone slab perhaps
thirty thousand years earlier by the primitive men who used
it as a sepulcher. The skeletons of seventeen persons (later
named Cro-Magnon men) were found within the cavern, but
physical anthropology was far from the thoughts of the mayor
of Aurignac. He decided they had come by their death
"through causes unknown" and accorded them a Christian
burial in the parish cemetery.

However, the matter was not to end there. Just as a lawyer
of Lewes discovered Piltdown Man more than half a century
later, so did a lawyer, Monsieur Lartet, figure prominently in
the history of Cro-Magnon man. In 1860 he visited the cave at
Aurignac, dug up its undisturbed floor, and found remains of
the cave bear, lion, and hyena, as well as mammoth, woolly
rhinoceros, giant stag, and other mammals. Most of the bones
had been broken to extract the marrow and many were
charred. Fire hearths, stone implements, necklaces of shell and
teeth and ivory carvings lay buried in the platform at the entrance to the cavern. But the human remains were completely
lost and there was no way to determine to what race they belonged. Nevertheless, the culture which was identical with that
of the Paviland cave, Kent's Cavern, and the Meuse River
grottoes received the name "Aurignacian" after the village of
Aurignac.

Lawyer Lartet's son, Louis, inherited his father's enthusiasm for archaeology and to him belongs the credit for first identifying the authors of the "Aurignacian culture." When, in 1868, workmen constructing a railroad bed near a rock shelter at Cro-Magnon, Les Eyzies, Department of Dordogne, exposed fire hearths, reindeer bones, stone artifacts, and the skeleton of an old man and four other individuals, Louis Lartet took charge. Before long the remains were recognized as an extinct type of modern human, henceforth to be known as Cro-Magnon Man. Sometimes he is called Aurignacian Man after his stone industry, just as the Neanderthals are often referred to as Mousterian men.

The initial discovery of Aurignacian Man stimulated search for his remains throughout Europe and a detailed study of his culture. More than a hundred individuals were discovered. It would be pointless for me to list them all. I must speak, however, of the study conducted by the Prince of Monaco of the caves near Menton on the French Riviera.

The Prince was imbued with deep scientific interest, particularly in oceanography, and I remember with what enthusiasm he conducted me through his Museum at Monaco many years ago. He had become greatly interested in the caves which open on the south face of the red rocks of Grimaldi, sixty feet above the sea where Aurignacian Man had lived at the close of the Old Stone Age. He determined to investigate them with the aid of the best authorities on primitive man available. To that end he collected a distinguished group of French scientists. They began work in 1895 and during the next seven years explored seven large caves and rock shelters.

Remains of fifteen individuals were disinterred but only nine were in a condition possible for detailed study. In the *Grotte des Enfants,* thirty-three feet of deposits were removed, revealing ten floors of habitation. The lowest layer produced the Mousterian implements of Neanderthal Man and the upper nine those of Aurignacian culture, with the characteristic accompanying fauna except for woolly rhinoceros and mammoth. Apparently these two ice-loving mammals did not vacation on the Riviera.

In the third level, nine feet below the surface, the skeletons of two young children were uncovered. From them the grotto takes its name. On the eighth level a man 6 feet $2\frac{1}{2}$ inches tall was lying on his back in an obvious grave surrounded by ornaments of shells and teeth. The ninth level yielded two skeletons; one a woman and the other a boy of sixteen, whose bones had been stained with red ochre. These individuals, probably mother and son, started a hot controversy among European anthropologists, for they were supposed to present negroid characters. Subsequently it has been shown that this idea has little foundation in fact.

The *Grotte des Enfants* demonstrates how a single desirable cave had been used during thousands of years as a dwelling by prehistoric people, with periods of non-habitation, from Neanderthal times through successive generations up to the close of the Old Stone Age.

At the time Cro-Magnon Man invaded Europe, the British Isles were connected and broadly united to the Continent. The Baltic Sea was a great fresh-water lake; Europe and Africa were joined by land bridges across the Mediterranean. It was an enticing country which he entered. The maximum of the Fourth Glacial period had passed and the climate was becoming dry and stimulating with temperate, if not warm, summers. Already the ice fields had withdrawn to the mountains, but the glacial period had not ended, for during the next centuries three new lesser advances of ice drove men back into their caves. But each cold period was less rigorous than the last and the warm intervals continued longer.

The steppes, meadows, and forests teemed with animals much like those of Mousterian times. Reindeer was the most abundant animal, but the mammoth, woolly rhinoceros, and musk ox still lingered along the edge of the ice. Later their places were taken by the warmer climate animals such as the bison, horse, stag, giant deer or "Irish elk," the cave lion, cave bear, and cave hyena.

Cro-Magnon men came to Europe following the game because they were inherently hunters and explorers. Probably the world has never seen a physical type better fitted for the nomadic adventurous life they led. Part of the year, at least, they lived completely in the open, wandering far from the grottoes and caves to which they had to retire during the winter. The Solutreans, cousins of the typical Cro-Magnons, had a vast plains camp at Solutré, near Lyons, France, which they probably occupied during the summer. They were great lovers of horse meat, and the remains of one hundred thousand horses together with thirty-five thousand flint implements were discovered at this place, alone. There is no clear evidence, however, to show that they had domesticated the horse. That discovery probably was made later in the Far East and not in

Europe. These ancient hunters doubtless erected shelters which they occupied summer after summer at places most favorable for game and fish. Indeed signs called "tectiforms" on the walls of caves may indicate that they built log huts roofed

Giant Deer or "Irish Elk"

After Painting by Charles R. Knight
COURTESY OF CHICAGO NATURAL HISTORY MUSEUM

with hides, although some authorities believe they are pictures of game traps.

Of course Cro-Magnon Man and his cousins did not continue to exist throughout twenty-five or thirty thousand years without changes in their culture and physical type. As a matter of fact, archaeologists recognize three major divisions of the late

Palaeolithic period—Aurignacian, Solutrean, and Magdalenian. The first is characterized by the typical Cro-Magnons, with a culture which followed and gradually emerged from the cruder Mousterian technique of Neanderthal Man. The tools are lighter, smaller, and more finely worked than the Mousterian, and bone was first used for wedges, lance points, pins, needles, awls, beads, and pendants.

In the Solutrean, flint work reached its highest development. By pressure chipping the Solutreans were able to take off long narrow flakes of flint. Some implements are twelve to fourteen inches long, so thin they are actually translucent and worked on both sides. The narrow blades are called "willow leaf," and the broad ones "laurel leaf." They also made beautiful spearheads and tools of great variety. Its geographical distribution suggests that it came from the East, perhaps from the plains of Russia and Western Siberia. The Solutreans were roundheaded people, but in the following stage, the Magdalenian, the physical type is slender, with well-shaped heads and attractive features. Although it recalls the Cro-Magnon, the men were by no means as tall and powerful. During this period cold and wet snow compelled the people to live in the entrances of caves and under rock shelters. Forests overgrew the lowlands of Western Europe, interspersed with meadows and swamps, and tundra bordered the ice fields. Reindeer and horses furnished the Magdalenians their principal food but other forest and steppe animals were abundant. The mammoth and woolly rhinoceros disappeared after the beginning of the period.

It was at this time that cave art reached its highest development, but skill in stone work declined, probably because the

Magdalenians discovered that bone and deer antlers were more easily worked and sufficiently durable for their needs. They had a great assortment of harpoons, spears, daggers, saws, drills, fish hooks, needles, ivory buttons, pendants, and amulets; in addition they invented the spear thrower. The variety of needles naturally indicates thread for which they could have used tendons and plant fibers. Also the buttons must have fastened clothes. While the Neanderthals probably draped skins about their bodies, the late Old Stone Age people undoubtedly wore garments stitched together. Moreover, the great abundance of scrapers shows that they worked and softened hides. Even though they knew how to prepare clay for modeling, there is no evidence that they used it for pottery. Neither did they domesticate any animal or plant. At the end of the Old Stone Age the Magdalenians either disappeared or became so mixed with other types that they seemed to disappear. At any rate, with them passed the great era of prehistoric art which has made them famous.

One of the most dramatic and important discoveries in human prehistory was made in the very center of Europe—in the old province of Moravia in Czechoslovakia, in 1924. It was as rich in surprises, and as illuminating, as the unveiling of the Tomb of Tutankhamen or the excavation of Pompeii. But instead of a mere thirteen centuries, the story unfolded at Predmost, in Moravia, goes back perhaps twenty-five thousand years to the time when glaciers were retreating slowly from the face of Europe; when mammoths, musk ox, and reindeer were the beef cattle of the day, and the cave lion, the cave hyena, and the cave bear were the sworn enemies of man and beast. Never before has so complete a revelation been made of the life led by our ancestors during the Ice Age—those men and women whose blood runs in our own veins.

In Moravia an amphitheater of hills is broken by the valley of the Becva, through which today runs the main railway line from Warsaw to Vienna. In Old Stone Age times, the same route served migrating herds of game as a gateway to the flat plains of Silesia and Poland. Probably, too, it was the highway which our own ancestors followed from Asia to the west of Europe. At the southern entrance to the pass rises a rugged mass of limestone, sheltering the village of Predmost, nestled against its base. Establishing their winter homes in the caves and rock shelters of the surrounding hills, mammoth hunters camped on the valley floor when the game passed through. Tens of thousands of primitive folk swarmed on the plains. There, century after century, they lived and hunted and died. Why they left, no one knows, but as the years went by a thick blanket of wind-blown loess sifted over their desert campground just as Pompeii was covered by the ashes of Vesuvius. This fine brown silt, which cuts like cheese, in some places reaches a depth of sixty-five feet. As far back as 1571, the historian Blahoslav records the bones of "giants" buried in the loess and in 1884 Professor Maska unearthed mammoth remains, charcoal, and stone implements at the foot of the limestone cliff.

Ten years later he made a great discovery—a wonderful tomb buried deep beneath the loess in which twenty individuals had been interred: twelve adults, and eight children of varying ages. Near one child lay a beautiful necklace of Arctic fox teeth; beside another the skull of a fox. Not all of the skeletons were intact. Half of them had been disturbed and broken, but the others were excellently preserved. Obviously it was a family sepulcher in which burials had been made at different times. The tomb was oval in shape, thirteen feet long by seven and one-half feet wide. One side was walled with upright mammoth shoulder blades; the other with lower jaws of the same great animal. A roof of flat stones protected the human remains from predatory beasts.

The skeletons tell a revealing story. They were a powerful, big-brained, large-headed people, those ancient hunters of Moravia! The men averaged 5 feet 7 inches in height and the women 5 feet four. Sir Arthur Keith says that in all the features of the skull and face they were true primitive Europeans. They most resembled their contemporaries in France, the Cro-Magnons. Although not as tall, the two were racial cousins and both represented the ancestral types of the men of Europe in the closing days of the Ice Age. Duplicates of the female skulls which Keith studied could easily be found among the living inhabitants of Scandinavia and Britain. Their faces were regularly formed and showed none of the robust and primitive features seen in the males. Sir Arthur remarks that we need not be surprised at this strong sexual differentiation for in all races of mankind the women tend much more than the men to retain the features of childhood and youth.

After the discovery of the tomb, in 1894, the excavations at Predmost suffered a long eclipse. Not until thirty years later did systematic work begin again, and then, as is so frequently the case, the real extent of the campsite was revealed by a commercial project. Loess for building bricks was being dug from the Predmost beds. Workmen found enormous numbers of mammoth and other bones, tools, hearths, and ornaments of bone, stone, and ivory. The remains all lay in a definite stratum in the valley, three to fourteen feet below the surface. Dr. Karl Absolon was put in charge of the archaeological work by the Czechoslovakian Government, and collected thousands of specimens for the Brunn Museum. In 1928 he discovered a hearth above which lay a human skeleton. The skull was missing and the bones were deeply scarred by knife cuts—grim evidence that the man had been cooked and eaten at that very spot.

Dr. Absolon undertook a systematic excavation of another great site, about a thousand acres in extent, some sixty miles from Predmost. He employed a plan similar to that used in uncovering the buried city of Pompeii. The whole area was divided into square meters. The contents of each section were carefully described, drawn, and photographed as the blanketing loess was removed and the ancient floor exposed. Only the upper three-quarters of the specimens were uncovered, leaving them still embedded in the earth. Then these were removed in great blocks, placed together in the Museum, and the ground plan of the settlement reconstructed.

It was far from a haphazard village; these were a people who preferred order to chaos. Certain areas had been designated as living quarters. In front of tents, or huts, pitched side by side, were extensive fireplaces. Not far away huge refuse pits contained the bones of mammoth, rhinoceros, lion, horse, reindeer, and Arctic fox, heaped in orderly arrangement. Behind the tents, three piles of mammoth tusks had been stacked like cordwood, separated by a narrow path. At one side was an enormous field of pelvic bones and another of lower jaws. Mammoth thigh bones, arranged in a half-circle, their ends charred, gave the archaeologists food for thought. They finally decided these were "fire logs." As the bones heated the fat exuded, keeping the fire alight. Few mammoth skulls remained intact. Evidently brains were an especial delicacy—the bigger the better!

Dr. Absolon discovered a workshop where the primitive artisans made their tools. A large stone anvil and a smaller one, pitted from long use, stone hammers and quantities of jasper flakes, cores and finished implements came to light. An artists's laboratory was not far away. Here were statuettes made from an unusual matrix. Charred and powdered bones had been mixed with clay to form a modeling paste. Some were completed, others only half made, and cakes of the raw material, showing traces of kneading, lay upon the ground. The statuettes represented animals, an owl, and a few men and women. One was an especially well-modeled female figurine. Dr. Absolon calls it his "Venus." Although much more artistic than most Palaeolithic human effigies, with the long pendant breasts it can hardly be described as beautiful. It seems very strange that the artists, with all their intelligence and inventive genius, did not recognize the use of clay for pots and bowls. But it was long after Palaeolithic times that the baking of clay was first discovered.

At Vestonice, a spring was exposed twenty feet below the surface of the loess. Dr. Absolon is certain this must have played an important part in the life of the Mammoth Hunters. Doubtless they came here to wash their meat and for drinking water. No trace of ashes existed, but stone plates, unburned mammoth bones, teeth, and a workshop for stone implements were uncovered.

It requires but little imagination to visualize this settlement of the Mammoth Hunters as it functioned twenty-five thousand years ago. In the background is a long row of tents, or huts, surrounded by orderly heaps of bones, like the wood-piles on a New England farm. Clustered about a fire, kept alight by the fat of mammoth thigh bones, sit powerful men dressed in skins, gnawing at great hunks of roasted meat. A girl, her face rouged with red ochre, and wearing a necklace of fox teeth, brings them water from the spring in a leather bucket. At one side artists of the tribe fashion chunks of flint into scrapers and knives or bind spear points to shafts of wood. At another fire women are sewing skins with bone needles and thread of reindeer sinews or plant fibers, working hides with stone scrapers, rouging their faces, and nursing crying babies. The picture might be that of any aboriginal people today living on the plains in an open camp.

The ornaments, tools, weapons, and household utensils, even spoons and a two-pronged fork of bone, reveal an organized civilization in which religion, magic, taboo, and art figure as in that of living primitive tribes. Animals they drew with life-like accuracy, but strangely enough none of the old Stone Age artists seemed to appreciate the beauty of the human figure, or else taboo prevented them from reproducing it with accuracy. Enormous buttocks, enlarged breasts, and expanded hips characterized all the sculpture or etching of women in their art. Usually the faces are blank, or barely outlined. Dr. Absolon discovered the half of a human skull with bevelled edges that obviously had served either as a drinking cup or a lamp. This is reminiscent of the Tibetans who use a skull top in a similar way during religious ceremonies.

Although almost every phase of the Predmost culture was revealed, only twenty or more human skeletons came to light. Obviously the dead were buried in tombs some distance from the camp, but further exploration will doubtless reveal the sepulchers. Virtually all the bodies discovered had been flexed and stained with red ochre.

The Predmost people, and indeed all those of later Old Stone Age times, were mighty hunters. The beasts they had to kill were the most formidable the world has ever known. A mammoth, a woolly rhinoceros, or a cave bear could not be attacked successfully without due thought and plan. Throwing spears at the vast bulk of a mammoth would do no more than send him into a rage, even though his body bristled with darts like an animated pincushion. So the Predmost hunters resorted to pitfalls. We know this is true, for Dr. Absolon has discovered deep depressions in the valley floor which undoubtedly were animal traps. Moreover, huge pear-shaped stones, some weighing more than a hundred pounds, lead him to believe that the men encased them in leather thongs and dropped them on the heads of entombed mammoths. That they were successful in their hunting, the remains of more than one hundred thousand mammoths testify. None of the great animals of the day—the woolly rhinoceros, the mammoth, the cave bear, or the cave lion—were able to compete with the Wise Man of the Old Stone Age. Already he had become the Lord of All the Earth.

The story of the Moravian Mammoth Hunters has been only partly told. Thousands of yards in this treasure house of pre-history still remain to be exposed. War has stopped the work. Politics and archaeology do not mix. But it is a comforting

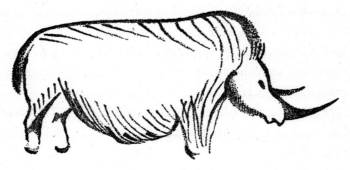

Rock Painting of Woolly Rhinoceros in Cavern of Font de Gaume

COURTESY OF THE AMERICAN MUSEUM OF NATURAL HISTORY

thought that although tanks have rumbled over the land and armies tread the valley, the thick layer of wind-blown loess still preserves the unread chapters from the ravages of human strife even as it has done for thirty centuries.

Undoubtedly the birth of art in the Old Stone Age was a direct result of cave life. The increasing cold and storms forced primitive men to remain within their shelters many days of the year. Thus they had leisure for contemplation, interchange of ideas, and the development of imagination along esthetic and mystical lines. While roaming the meadows and forests, intent upon the chase, their thoughts were only those of physical existence and comfort. As a present-day comparison, I think of the Mongols who wander over the plains at the dictation of the grazing for their flocks and herds. They lead a nomadic life almost completely in the open, comparable to the men of the warm period of the Old Stone Age. Of necessity their household possessions must be kept to the absolute minimum; seldom do they remain within their felt tent an entire day. Thus even in the years when Genghis Khan ruled most of the then known world, the Mongols had no art. Yet to the south of them, the static and gregarious Chinese were far advanced in art, philosophy, and material culture.

Almost every writer becomes lyrical over the painting and sculpture of the Old Stone Age. Not so Professor Hooton. He considers it to be much over-rated. While he admits there were some excellent drawings and engravings in the caves of France and Spain, he believes most of it was mediocre or even bad. He says: "The enthusiasm of students of prehistory has outstripped their sense of values in the estimate placed upon these attempts at art." (1936, p. 371) Not being an artist myself I wouldn't know how good it is from a purely technical standpoint. But I have discussed the matter with several artists, among them the celebrated painter of prehistoric animals and man, Charles R. Knight, who has visited many of the caves in France and Spain. He agrees with the others, that not all the paintings and sculptures have equal merit, but that some are excellent even judged by modern standards. Neither do all present-day artists have like talent. Some are bad, others good, and a very few outstanding. Why should primitive artists all have been Titians? When one remembers that the Aurignacians were only one stage removed from the crude Neanderthals; that for the first time men had shown other than physical instincts; that esthetic appreciation had at last become so definitely a part of the human mind that it called for expression in painting and sculpture; that they began at the *very beginning* with no inheritance or history of art on which to build, no background of old masters for study of technique, it seems to me its importance can hardly be overestimated or it be praised too highly. It may not all be very good art, but the worst is immeasurably better than the nothing at all that preceded or immediately followed it. Moreover, the drawings of the cave man were executed under extraordinary difficulties. He had no models to pose for him—all his subjects were drawn from memory. There was no carefully arranged studio with a uniform north light. Instead, the primitive artist worked in the uncertain flare of torches or stone lamps of smoking animal fat. He had no modern scaffolding to enable him to paint in comfort on the ceiling of his cave, but paint he did and it must have been most arduous. He had to discover everything about the medium in which he worked. There was no previous experience upon which to draw. With him it was trial and error.

Painting had its inception in Aurignacian times by the simple outlining of the contour of the hand pressed against the wall, and only engraving or flat wash was used. In the Solutrean period, bas-relief sculpture advanced, while painting suffered an arrested development but reappeared again vigorously with the Magdalenians who employed color—yellow, red, brown, and black. Dr. Raymond Murray remarks that "their colors, made from minerals which seem to have been mixed with fats by some unknown process, were so lasting that modern chemists are at a loss to explain them. A paint

Stationary Polychrome Bison in Cave at Altamira, Spain

COURTESY OF AMERICAN MUSEUM OF NATURAL HISTORY

chemist told the writer that paint manufacturers would like to learn the secret of these artists of over ten thousand years ago and then lock it up, for if it were used commercially it would 'ruin the paint business.' " (1943, p. 156)

In the American Museum of Natural History we have faithful reproductions of the bison painted on the roof of the cave of Altamira in the Spanish Pyrenees. The colors are amaz-

ingly brilliant; probably there has been but little fading during
the thousands of years since their first application to the surface of the rock. This is partly due to the Stygian darkness
and the uniform temperature of the caverns. Ochre and oxide
of manganese were the pigments most frequently employed
by the Magdalenians. The artist prepared them by grinding
and mixing them with animal fat. The paints were kept in
big bone tubes and skulls. Probably brushes were made of
fibrous wood or possibly hair. Sometimes too they employed
crayons whittled from pieces of ochre or manganese. Not only
have the pigments themselves been found, but also pestles for
grinding and palettes of stone and bone, some of them still
daubed with red.

Just why the primitive artists sought the most remote
caverns, some of them exceedingly difficult of access, for their
engraving, painting, and sculpture is a matter of some speculation. The decorated parts of the caves show no signs of having been used for residence. Most authorities agree that the
incentive for Stone Age art grew out of a belief in magic, or
superstition. Professor Osborn believes that the sculptured
female bison awaiting the bull in the cave of Tuc d'Audoubert
expresses the idea of fecundity. Also in the *Trois Frères* cavern
is a picture of a male reindeer pursuing a female. Female
human figures predominate in statuettes and many of them
are pregnant. Thus by drawing or modeling the animals they
preferred for food, male and female together, it was hoped
the supply might increase. Little of the cave art is concerned
with non-edible beasts, but wolf and lion are present. On the
other hand, many of the paintings show game animals rid-

dled with punctures as if from arrows. Probably the belief, held by certain living primitive tribes, that piercing the picture of an animal in a vital spot insured its easy capture, originated with these early hunters. The African voodoo, in which a spell is cast over an enemy by mutilating some part of his body represented in a figurine, is another ancient superstition possibly of similar origin.

Before I close this chapter, I must mention again the primitive humans who lived on "Dragon Bone Hill" at Choukoutien, where Peking Man dwelt so many centuries ago. They were a peculiar group of Upper Stone Age people, occupying the Western Hills of North China at the same time that the Aurignacians were spreading over Western Europe, and had a corresponding culture; moreover, they are the earliest representatives of modern men yet found on the continent of East Asia.

Their cave was separated from that of Peking Man during his occupation but opened into it much later during Upper Palaeolithic times. The deposit consists of gray loam mixed with fragmentary bits of limestone and is quite unlike that of the Peking Man cavern.

Although the cave was discovered in 1930, it was not until 1933, after I had left Peking, that the excavation began, so I did not see it personally. Dr. Weidenreich tells me that the incomplete skeletons of seven individuals were unearthed together with many stone and bone implements and ornaments; also thousands of bones of tiger, ostrich, sika deer, and hare. Apparently this was not a dwelling cave, but rather a sepulcher, for the bones are mixed and four of the skulls show injuries resulting from blows while the individuals still lived. Dr. Weidenreich thinks it possible that some of the people were victims of a sudden attack and their bodies were dismembered and thrown into the cave.

The skeletons are those of two women, two men, one youth, and two children; of the last, one is about five years old and the other perhaps a baby yet unborn. The strange thing about this discovery is that each of the skulls seems to represent a different type of modern man. Dr. Weidenreich says (1938–39) that one resembles the Mongolian, another is more Melanesoid, and a third is Eskimoid. He can see no direct relation between Peking Man and these Upper Cave people, nor do they shed any light on the origin of the Chinese. They do show, however, that even in the earliest appearance of modern man in Asia differentiation into racial types was already an accomplished fact.

CHAPTER THIRTEEN

Drama and Adventure in Cave Exploration

WHILE RIDING WITH Professor Henry Fairfield Osborn across the barren reaches of the Gobi Desert in 1923, he told me a fascinating story of cave exploration in which three young French boys figured as the heroes. Only two years earlier he had visited France for the second time to examine the rock engravings and sculpture of Old Stone Age man in the caverns of the Pyrenees and Dordogne. His host was the Comte de Bégouen, on whose estate, near Saint Girons, the discoveries were made. From the Comte he heard the story.

A rivulet runs out of the mouth of a cave called the Tuc d'Audoubert. In 1912 the Comte's sons built a tiny boat in which they pushed along the stream for a distance of two hundred feet to enter a gallery covered with mural etchings made perhaps fifteen thousand years ago. The discovery was a sensation in the archaeological world. Filled with enthusiasm, the boys searched for other galleries in the cave. It was not until later, however, that they found an aperture in one side almost concealed among fallen rocks. They could barely worm their small bodies through the hole into a narrow defile leading upward. Crawling on their stomachs, twisting and turning, they at last emerged into a breath-taking chamber of stalactites—a chapel of purest white. Weird drape-like hangings, spears of calcite, slender columns and lacework basins filled with silent pools of water reflected the torch light in colors of rose, blue, and emerald green. As in a scene from fairyland they could imagine tiny winged creatures dancing on the crystal trees or swinging in play from the fantastic hangings in the shadows of the roof. On the floor lay several skulls of the great cave bear.

From this chamber of beauty, passages led in half a dozen directions, each one enticing the boys to follow: a labyrinth in which they might become lost and wander endlessly seeking a road to freedom. Pushing upward, squeezing around narrow corners, crawling inch by inch through openings where the roof pressed down, wriggling and twisting, their bodies scratched and clothes torn, they emerged at last into a stately hall, fifty feet long, thirty feet wide, and twelve feet high. Silent with awe, the three young French boys flashed their torches around the room. At the end of the chamber lay a circle of stones, a mystic symbol where strange rites may have been practiced by the men who first entered this chamber fifteen thousand years ago. But wonder of all wonders, against a great mass of clay leaned the modeled figures of two massive bison, a bull behind, a cow leading! Preserved by the moisture of the cave, the clay was still soft to the touch, almost as fresh as when the primitive artist molded it with strong, sure strokes into the form of the animals he knew so well. The surface is smooth but shows traces of the sculptor's hand; thumb marks remain on the hair hanging from the neck. Rolls of kneaded clay still retain the impressions of the workman's fingers. Two other bison silhouettes are deeply incised in the clay, and the imprints of the artist's feet and the claws

Sculptured Bison Discovered by the Three Brothers
in the Cave of Tuc d'Audoubert

COURTESY OF AMERICAN MUSEUM OF NATURAL HISTORY

of cave bears show as plainly as though they had been made the day before.

Opening from the bison hall is a small chamber where the boys discovered impressions of delicate hands and feet deeply pressed into the clay and covered by a thin veneer of lime. Little people the artists seemed to have been, of short stature with fine extremities. The heels are deeply dug into the matrix of the floor and sinuous tracks subsequently suggested the name *Salle de Danse,* although there is no real evidence that it was used for such a purpose. More probably the footprints were made while the sculptor was gathering modeling clay.

But to return to the three brothers. Filled with excitement,

Model of the Castillo Cave Showing Primitive Artists at Work

Courtesy of American Museum of Natural History

the boys made their way out of the cavern and ran to report the discovery to their father. The Comte was as excited as his sons. Professor Osborn said with admiration, "Never can I understand how he negotiated the journey through those tortuous passages! He is not thin—in fact I should call him

198

decidedly portly—and yet he got through. Of course, they took picks and shovels to break down the impossible corners and enlarge the narrowest corridors, but it was a feat of which any man could well be proud. When I visited it, the trip was arduous enough, but by that time ladders had been installed and the worst places enlarged. Still it was difficult—very difficult."

Eventually the cavern became a Mecca for the world's most distinguished archaeologists. The sculptures were studied and photographed and a minute examination made of every foot of the cave's interior. Near the entrance were small heaps of implements and bones, including skulls of the cave bear, so it was believed that a part of the cavern had been inhabited at various periods. But the interior hall of sculpture may never have been visited again after the artist left it when his work was done.

The three Bégouen brothers had made one of the greatest discoveries in prehistoric archaeology; they had been the first modern human beings to gaze upon the work and footprints of those men of the Old Stone Age who lived one hundred and fifty centuries before the birth of Christ. The drama of their exploration could seldom, if ever, be enacted again.

But the young Frenchmen had no thought of resting on their laurels. Only a short time after discovering the *Salle des Bisons,* they decided to investigate a strange chimney in the top of a limestone hill not far from the Tuc d'Audoubert, where air currents swept up from the interior of a cavern. Although it had long been known to the peasants of the vicinity, no one had the courage to do more than peer into its black depths. It was a hazardous undertaking but the boys got themselves let down by a rope into a new cave with a different art technique of a different period, early Magdalenian. Instead of sculptures, here were etchings. The walls and ceiling of the cavern, since time immemorial had been overlaid with a thin brown veneer, underneath which lay the primeval white limestone. By scratching through the brown layer, the primitive artists drew outlines of reindeer, horses, mammoths, cave bears, panthers, lions, stags, and bison. Most abundant of all was the last, evidently because it was the most prized food animal of the time. The etchings were done with such skill and care that it is even possible to identify the species of the subjects. Every available surface of the cavern was decorated, the ceiling as well as the walls.

Again the Comte squeezed his stalwart form through the chimney and into the narrow passages to verify the report of his sons. The cavern was appropriately called *Les Trois Frères* in honor of the boys. In the last chamber was a remarkable figure subsequently named the "Sorcerer." Apparently it portrays what our American Indians call a "Medicine Man," or magician. The face wears the mask and ears of a fox, and a long pointed beard; the head is surmounted by the horns of a stag, the arms appear to be covered with the skin of a bear, the legs are striped and the bushy tail of a fox hangs from the figure's rear. That this "medicine man" was not a local tribal conception is shown by its close resemblance to an etching found in the grotto of Lourdes in the eastern Pyrenees. Probably it had widespread magical significance among the people of the time.

Professor Osborn told me how impressed he was by the accuracy of the animal drawings in proportions and detail and of the anatomical truth in the sculptured bison. To his mind they are the works of true artists with all the imagination and feeling of men of genius.

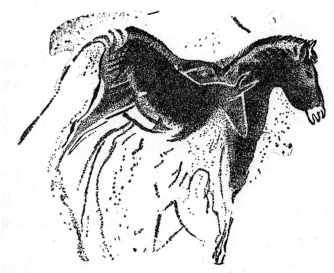

Painting of a Horse with a Superimposed Hind from the Cave at Altamira, Spain

COURTESY OF THE AMERICAN MUSEUM OF NATURAL HISTORY

Other children have been responsible for several of the great cave discoveries. In 1879 a Spanish nobleman, Marcellino de Sautuola, was investigating caves near his home in Santander accompanied by his small daughter. While digging for artifacts in the vestibule of the Cueva de Altamira, the child began an exploration on her own account. She wandered into a huge chamber to the left of the entrance and suddenly cried, *"Toros! Toros!"* (bulls), pointing to the ceiling. Her amazed father saw a herd of bulls, deer, horses, boars and other animals painted upon the roof of the cave. Some were outline drawings in black, others in red wash, and still more in polychromes. In the best paintings the silhouettes were done in black with free masterful strokes, the body color smeared on with paste graduated to half-tones and the details supplied with a brush. The walls and ceilings of many chambers in the vast cavern were decorated with some of the finest examples of Magdalenian art thus far known.

Sautuola immediately made his discovery available to the scientific world, but 1879 was not 1914 so far as the progress of archaeology was concerned. The nobleman's presentation was received with profound skepticism by the Archaeological Congress of 1897. The art was too good, the colors too fresh, and the paintings too well preserved to convince them that fifteen thousand years had elapsed since their execution. It was not until 1901, after similar murals had been found in other caves, that their antiquity was finally admitted.

Another child made himself famous by discovering a great gallery of prehistoric paintings in the Department of Lot, in southern France. David, a boy of fourteen, had been inspired by the Abbé Lemozi, a country curé and an enthusiastic archaeologist, with the adventure and romance of cave exploration. On a Thursday in July 1922, he resolved to visit alone a certain hole near a clump of oak trees on his father's property. The opening was narrow but David was as lithe and slender as a willow wand. He wriggled through the entrance and up a short ascent along a passage sloping at an angle of forty-five degrees into utter blackness. He lighted a candle and traversed a gallery which grew wider as he advanced. At last he reached a platform where the roof rose higher and the area increased. Evidently there was a larger gallery beyond.

David was tremendously excited. He ran back to his father who immediately informed the Abbé Lemozi. Together the priest and the boy explored the cavern. Following a passage to the right, they soon reached a point where the roof was so low that the Abbé had to crawl. Suddenly, however, the tunnel expanded and, turning, opened into a vast hall adorned with fantastic stalactites and stalagmites. Symmetrical folds of purest white draped the ceiling; the walls held brackets and rounded knobs like giant crystal mushrooms and fountain basins; the floor seemed paved with gleaming Parian marble.

A passage to the left led the explorers into a tunnel so low that they had to wriggle forward stretched at full length like reptiles. At last it widened sufficiently so that they could walk upright with lowered heads for about a hundred yards; then came another ordeal of crawling on their stomachs. Having eventually squeezed through, they scrambled over a pile of debris to stand in awe before massive pillars guarding the entrance to another majestic hall, similar to the first except that the crystal drapes were tinged with red. A new gallery, long and winding, splendidly hung with statuettes, led to the marvel of the place—the two terminal halls.

After a month the exploration was resumed. A new tunnel, where the boy and priest were almost overcome by poisonous gases, led them to an immense gallery nearly four hundred

feet long by thirty-six feet wide. There the walls were almost
clear of stalactites but decorated with forty murals engraved
or painted in black and red. Mammoths, bison, horses, and
fish were represented and ten detached silhouettes of human
hands done in red ochre. All the pictures were starred with

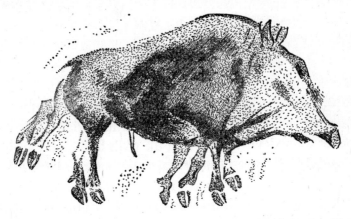

Walking Wild Boar Painted over an Earlier Sketch in the Cave
of Altamira, Spain

COURTESY OF THE AMERICAN MUSEUM OF NATURAL HISTORY

symbols, seemingly hieroglyphic. Not a sign of implements
could be found but there were remains of animal bones and
traces of footprints in the hardened clay. The ceiling, some
twenty-three feet above the floor, was engraved with inter-
lacing designs. How did the primitive artists reach the ceiling
without scaffolding and with only oil lamps for light? It is
an interesting speculation. Perhaps, after all, they knew more
about engineering than we suspect.

The Abbé Lemozi does not believe that the drawings are

all of the same period. He regards most of them as a little earlier than the Magdalenian paintings of Eyzies.

The daring of all other cave explorers is far eclipsed by that of a young Frenchman, Norbet Casteret, in 1923. Because he was a champion swimmer and diver as well as an enthusiastic archaeologist, he was enabled to make one of the most remarkable discoveries in cave art. His feat is one of the outstanding adventures in prehistoric research.

In the beautiful little commune of Montespan in the foot-hills of the Pyrenees, a cave runs right through a wooded knoll. Actually it is a subterranean stream three-quarters of a mile long. The cave is only a short distance from the famous caverns of Aurignac, Tourasse, Marsoulas, and Tarte; more-over, seventeen and one-half miles away lies the Tuc d'Audou-bert where the Comte Bégouen's sons discovered the magnifi-cent sculptured bison in 1912.

No one had dared explore the cave for at several points water rose above the roof, forming dangerous "pipes." The diffi-culties appealed to Norbet Casteret. Equipped with candles and matches in a rubber bag and dressed only in bathing trunks, he dove through the icy water literally into the un-known. Alternately diving, swimming, and wading, he traversed the whole length of the cavern. Halls and passages opened off the stream, some of them of vast extent. One majestic theater, seven hundred and fifty feet long, contained an art gallery where paintings of bison, wild horses, reindeer, stags, mammoths, hyenas, and other animals made a beautiful mural decoration.

But most interesting of all were models in clay of bears,

horses, and tigers. Previously the only known prehistoric sculptures were the bisons of the Tuc d'Audoubert. A headless bear about three and one-half feet long, lying down, was the most spectacular model. Apparently the head never existed for it was replaced with the skull of a bear cub which had broken away and lay between the forefeet. The body, covered by lime accretions, showed the marks of thirty spear thrusts. About the bear on the floor Casteret identified twenty smaller models in bas-relief but so eroded by dripping water as to be unrecognizable. Affixed to a wall were three large figures of tigers and another bear pierced by jagged holes. Against a bank, with numerous clay balls molded by the artist's hands, rested half the body of a woman. Marks of human fingers covered the walls, and flint implements lay where they were discarded or forgotten.

Count Bégouen in commenting on Casteret's discovery draws particular attention to the sculptures, since no others had been discovered since the bisons of Tuc d'Audoubert. Undoubtedly they represent the same period—Magdalenian. He remarks that the figures are by no means as carefully executed as those in the cavern on his estate and that all are riddled with holes and gashes. Evidently they were meant to be destroyed like the animals which the tribe intended to hunt in the superstitious belief that beasts could be more easily killed by piercing their images with spear thrusts. The opposite is true of the Tuc d'Audoubert bison. These represented male and female and were carefully finished. Obviously the superstitious motive was to induce fecundity in the animals which furnished the favorite food of the primitive hunters.

Norbet Casteret did not rest on his laurels after discovering the great cave at Montespan. Near the village of Labastide, not far from Montespan, a stream runs out of a natural basin in the outlying spurs of the Pyrenees down a narrow ravine and disappears underground in a cavern known as la Spugue.

Cro-Magnon Artists in the Cavern of Font de Gaume

From Mural by Charles R. Knight in the American Museum of Natural History

Eventually it reappears at the town of Esparros. It was early April 1932, the stream was high and the water icy cold. Nevertheless Casteret decided to undertake his exploration. The first attempt nearly cost him his life. He encountered a layer of bad air given off by decaying vegetation and was nearly asphyxiated before he dragged himself out of the chamber.

After recovering his strength he climbed down another

precipitous part of the ravine and discovered a fine arcade at the bottom of a shaft. It was well that he had lighted his lamp before venturing into the inky blackness, because the floor suddenly dropped away into a deep abyss. Skirting the edge by crawling along a narrow shelf, he entered a small chamber. His light showed the walls to be covered with deeply incised etchings. Chief among the animals was the head of a roaring lion, muzzle thrown back and mouth open. It is beautifully executed and particularly interesting as being the only known representation of the extinct cave lion. Other sketches show a man in a mask, naked to the waist, with legs and body bent and his arms held horizontally in front. The figure is reminiscent of the "Sorcerer" in the cavern of the *Trois Frères* and of the "Suppliants" in the Altamira cave. At another level in the cavern the outline of a large horse filled in with red was drawn on the face of a great slab of rock evidently dislodged from the ceiling. This was the only use of color in the cave. At the extreme end of one gallery, on an earth platform, two large circles of stones enclosed ashes, calcined bones, jaws, teeth, and flint implements; obviously a place of ritual.

Casteret is convinced that the cavern of Labistide was a chapel or sanctuary where the primitive sorcerers devoted themselves to magical ceremonies connected with hunting, and not a studio where primitive artists withdrew to give their genius the advantage of peace and quiet.

THE DUNE DWELLERS
OF THE GOBI

Logically this book should end at the close of the Palaeolithic period when the Wise Men appeared upon the world's stage. But there was a transition period, the Mesolithic, before the use of pottery and polished implements ushered in the New Stone Age. Because we of the Central Asiatic Expedition discovered in the Gobi Desert a Mesolithic culture, which may prove to be of vast importance in human prehistory, particularly relating to North America, I am including the story in this chapter of drama and adventure.

We honestly thought that we were the original and only discoverers of the famous dinosaur eggs in 1923. But I must confess we were merely "also rans." A people we had never dreamed of had beaten us by the comfortable margin of fifteen or twenty thousand years. At the close of the Old Stone Age a primitive race lived in the Gobi, at the "Place of the Muddy Waters." Among other things they used bits of dinosaur egg shells as ornaments. They picked them up at the Flaming Cliffs where we got ours. We found in their "workshops" many pieces about half an inch square with a neat hole drilled in the middle like beads in a necklace used by some prehistoric debutante. Thus we cannot say any longer that we discovered the dinosaur eggs. But we did discover the discoverers of the eggs! Perhaps that is even better.

"The Dune Dwellers of Shabarakh Usu" is the name we gave the people who stole our glory. It is appropriate because

209

they lived in the sand dunes heaped by the wind about the roots of the salt-bush trees on the floor of the basin. Of course, fifteen or twenty thousand years has made a good many changes in the face of the country. To solve the problem of those changes, and to learn what manner of people the Dune Dwellers were from the scraps of evidence they left behind, was the job we had to do. The question of greatest interest when we began to work out the story was where they fitted into the mosaic of primitive European cultures. Did their weapons and tools represent a type known from Europe? If so, was it earlier than the European equivalent?

On the day our tents were pitched at the "Place of the Muddy Waters," J. B. Shackelford, the photographer, wandered off into the salt bushes. He had an instinct for finding interesting things and at dinner produced a pocketful of chipped flints. Dr. Nelson, our archaeologist, pronounced them to be of undoubted human origin. "Shack" said they were there in hundreds. The next morning, Nelson and I went out immediately after breakfast, followed by Drs. Berkey, Morris, and Loucks. We found an area of shifting sand blown into dunes topped by twisted salt-bush trees. Sculptured red bluffs marked the entrance to shallow valleys floored with sandstone where the wind had swept the loose sediment away. On the clean, hard surface of the rock, flakes of red jasper, slate, chalcedony, chert, and other stones were scattered like new-fallen snow. Pointed cores, neatly shaped by removal of slender prismatic flakes, tiny oblong and rounded scrapers, delicately worked drills, and a few arrowheads gave Nelson the first indications of the type of culture with which he had to deal.

We held a consultation. Where did the artifacts come from? Could they have been washed down from the surface? Those were the first questions to be answered. We must find flints actually embedded in the rocks and bones to date the deposit. Shortly after our consultation, I discovered a bit of egg shell of the giant ostrich *Struthiolithus*. The other men came on the run when I shouted. It was like "pay dirt" to a prospector for gold. This great bird existed in the Ice Age and if the makers of our flints were its contemporaries their culture must belong to that period. A few yards to the left, Morris found another fragment of egg shell with a neat round hole. This was human work. Nelson pronounced it one of the beads in a necklace. We were in a fever of excitement for the trail was getting hot. Nelson, the most conservative of all conservatives, was skipping about from place to place like a boy of sixteen. At last Dr. Berkey located half a dozen chipped flints securely embedded in the sandstone floor. By noon we had discovered many others and were satisfied that *some* of the artifacts had weathered out of the lowest level and not been washed down from the surface of the dunes. Still, until we found shells of the ostrich eggs, or fossil bones, actually in position, we could not be certain of the deposit's age.

An unlooked for complication entered when we began to discover fragments of pottery. It was primitive enough, to be sure, but a people who used such crude stone implements had no business to be making pottery! The problem became more interesting and more complicated every hour. So much so, indeed, that it was difficult to stick to our respective jobs. Everyone wanted to hunt artifacts.

The second day's work revealed dark spots in the lowest levels of the deposit. Evidently these were ancient fireplaces. Cross sections exposed layers of ash containing charcoal, flints, and burned stones. Soon we found square bits of dinosaur and ostrich egg shells embedded in the sandstone. This gave us pause. Then it was that we realized that the Dune Dwellers were the original discoverers of the dinosaur eggs. Dr. Loucks added another element of uncertainty to our problem by finding quantities of ostrich egg shells on the surface of the plateau. If the Dune Dwellers picked up bits of fossilized dinosaur egg shells at the Flaming Cliffs two or three miles away, and brought them to their workshops, they might have done the same with the ostrich eggs! Therefore, finding ostrich egg shells embedded with the flints would not prove that the Dune Dwellers were the bird's contemporaries.

After ten days of intensive work the evidence was well in hand and certain definite facts emerged. Nelson could state confidently that the site at Shabarakh Usu had been occupied by human beings for thousands of years. At least two successive cultures were represented. That of the lowest, and oldest, was late Palaeolithic, with no stone spear or arrow points or pottery. Above this a transition stage gradually developed into the Neolithic, characterized by stone arrow and spear points and crude pottery. Although the culture most closely resembles the Mesolithic Azilian of France and Spain, still it presents many unique aspects.

That the Dune Dwellers were widely distributed over Mongolia is certain. During all our explorations their artifacts were present wherever proper conditions existed. For camp sites they always selected the low basin and valleys where then, as now, ponds and sand dunes gave them water and fuel from the stunted salt-bush trees. I can imagine the dunes at Shabarakh Usu swarming with these strange people. Dressed in skins, probably living under crude shelters of hides or bushes, they hunted, worked, and loved, much as do the primitive aborigines of Australia today. Doubtless some members of the tribe developed unusual skill in fashioning implements of stone. These artisans did their work at certain spots where flakes of jasper and chalcedony now lie in thousands. "Workshops" we called them.

Dr. Loucks discovered a shallow valley where the flint chips were scattered over the floor in tens of thousands. In this single spot, Nelson collected fifteen thousand broken or partly finished implements, for of course the completed tools had been carried away for daily use.

The source of supply for the peculiar kind of stone needed by the Dune Dwellers puzzled us for a long time, since it did not occur at Shabarakh Usu. When returning near the end of the summer, we found it on a flat plain thirty-six miles from Shabarakh Usu. There tens of thousands of chunks of red jasper had been roughly flaked and left behind, together with some removed flakes. Nelson was not with us at the time and we were all greatly excited, for it seemed to us that these represented a pre-Chellean or Chellean culture, perhaps several hundred thousand years old. Nelson dampened our spirits considerably when he arrived. After spending several days studying the deposit and collecting specimens he stated positively that these coarse, rudely chipped pieces were only "test stones" discarded by the Dune Dwellers when they came to get materials. The primitive artisans picked out the best chunks after testing many others, and took them to their workshops to finish. It was like a modern lumber yard where the carpenter goes to select his wood.

Nelson started a hot controversy in camp. We were decidedly unwilling to abandon our idea of a new early Palaeolithic culture without a fight. Dr. Berkey returned with him to re-examine the site and the rest of us marshaled every argument we could think of to defend our theory. But Nelson demolished us one by one in the most cold-blooded way. After he had arranged a series of specimens in comparative rows, we finally had to admit that he was right. He was a professional archaeologist and we were only amateurs.

We hoped, up to the very last, to find burials where bones of the Dune Dwellers might be obtained. Skeletons, or skulls, would tell us what manner of men they were. We looked for them particularly in the vicinity of their hearths and permanent camping places, such as Shabarakh Usu. But not a trace of human bone could be found. Either their dead were not buried near the camps or the conditions were unfavorable for the preservation of bones. The latter is probably the correct reason as the fragmentary animal remains in the flint-bearing layers were badly preserved. Had we been able to discover caves, probably much more definite information could have been obtained. But caves are as scarce as hen's teeth in the region we explored. Although limestone is present in places, the erosion has not been of the type to produce caverns or even rock shelters. The Dune Dwellers must have lived in the open the entire year. Since at that time the winters were probably as cold as they are today, I don't wonder that they migrated!

Where did they go? As we expected might happen, a clue comes from Alaska. For some years the American Museum of Natural History has been conducting archaeological work in co-operation with University of Alaska at Fairbanks. In 1933 a superficial habitation site was discovered on the University campus and partly excavated during the following two years. Dr. Nelson says the station "lies on the eastern edge of 'College Hall' directly above and adjacent to a 75 foot bluff which descends steeply to the floor of the Tanana Valley. It appears to occupy a roundish, nearly level area about sixty feet in diameter, and exhibits cultural debris to a depth of about eighteen inches." (1937, p. 268)

Some eight hundred specimens, mostly fragmentary, were obtained from two sites, among which are end-scrapers, polygonal cores, together with the small prismatic flakes derived from them. These are identically the same as those of the Dune Dwellers of Mongolia. This suggests a "possible specific proof of culture between Asia and America." In recent years other Dune Dweller stations have been discovered in central Alaska, making the connection certain.

CHAPTER FOURTEEN

The First Americans

NOT A PARTICLE of evidence exists to show that man originated in America. After all, without seed one cannot grow a potato, and apparently the ape stock that gave rise to man was exclusively of Old World origin. Moreover, man did not arrive in America until late in geologic times. No positive traces of human occupation before the closing stage of the Ice Age have been discovered in either North or South America.

When man appeared he was already true *Homo sapiens.* Until less than twenty-five years ago any archaeologist would have asserted that the ancestral Indians, such as the Shell Mound people of the Pacific Coast and the Basket Makers of the Southwest, were the first inhabitants of North America and that they lived not long before the time of Christ; that our human history was only ancient to the extent of some three thousand years. What is three thousand years compared to the five hundred thousand or more assigned to the Java and Peking Men?

Of course, numerous "finds" had been made purporting to

be much older than the Shell Mound people and the Basket Makers. But none of them stood the acid test of expert investigation. In every case a good deal more than reasonable doubt existed and some were even proved to be fraudulent. Opinion that man was a very recent immigrant in America had become crystallized and dogmatic. Claims of great antiquity were rejected almost automatically.

There is, however, much to be said in extenuation of this "I'm from Missouri" attitude of American archaeologists. Some years ago, Florentine Ameghino, a well-known South American palaeontologist, more patriotic than scientific, claimed that man had originated in South America and vigorously defended his completely untenable position. In addition, a distinguished American geologist and Harvard professor, J. D. Whitney, thought he had demonstrated that the historic Indian culture could be traced back without modification to the Miocene period, a matter of some seven to fourteen million years. Also, C. C. Abbott, of Trenton, New Jersey, a Doctor of Medicine, tried to impress some natural rocks on the scientific world as manufactured implements dating from the glacial period.

There are only a few examples. As Dr. N. C. Nelson has well said: "If the romanticists had been left to carry on unhindered we would have had no science of archaeology. But this is not to deny that some of the archaeologists have been absurdly dogmatic." (From note to Author)

So the matter stood until 1926. Then a scientific bombshell was exploded by the late J. D. Figgins and his colleagues of the Colorado Museum of Natural History. They announced that in a fossil deposit at Folsom, New Mexico, parts of two stone dart points had been found in association with the bones of an extinct bison. A bison, moreover, not like those of our western plains. This particular bison had wide-spreading horns resembling those of a Texas steer and lived at the end of the Ice Age some twenty-five thousand years ago.

Figgins was a naturalist of repute but even that did not save him from the "pooh-poohs" of hard-boiled archaeologists. Suddenly to toss the date of man in America from three thousand years back to the close of the Ice Age was just too much. In short, the announcement was brushed aside as "another of those finds" hardly worth serious investigation. But Jesse Figgins was a Southerner who wouldn't be pooh-poohed. It made him mad. He went into the field the next year determined to show his critics. And he did. A dart point was discovered in the Folsom deposit actually embedded in the matrix between two ribs of the extinct bison. Figgins stopped work abruptly, leaving the exhibit partly uncovered. He telegraphed Dr. Barnum Brown, a distinguished palaeontologist of the American Museum, and Dr. Frank Roberts, Jr., of the Smithsonian Institution, urging them to take the first train to Folsom. They came, saw, and believed. In turn they themselves sent a few telegrams. Dr. A. V. Kidder, of the Carnegie Institution at Washington, arrived two days later. The block containing the ribs and the embedded dart point was removed intact and now reposes in the Colorado Museum of Natural History at Denver.

That winter the three visiting scientists, Drs. Brown, Kidder, and Roberts, jointly reported their verdict at the annual meeting of the American Anthropological Association at Andover, Mass. But even they were met with raised eyebrows and unconvinced stares from the archaeologists. It had always been assumed that the Shell Mound people and the Basket Makers were the earliest Americans, and they were determined to maintain that position in spite of hell and high water. But it

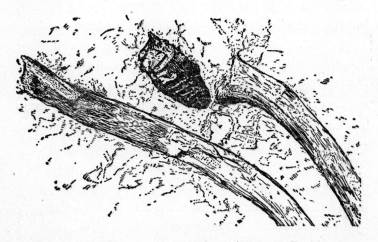

Block Containing Two Bison Ribs and Point in Position as Discovered

COURTESY OF THE AMERICAN MUSEUM OF NATURAL HISTORY

was a losing battle. The American Museum took a hand at the invitation of the Colorado Museum and co-operated the next year (1928) in further excavations. Twenty-three skeletons of the extinct bison were discovered associated with dart points. The skeletons all lacked the tail bones; apparently the tails had been stripped off with the hides when the animals were skinned. This, with other data, indicated that the

herd of bison had been rounded up and butchered at that very
spot.

Jesse Figgins was jubilant and Barnum Brown hardly less
so. Telegrams brought archaeologists, palaeontologists, and
geologists to the spot even from Europe, albeit somewhat
grudgingly. Their defenses were cracking all along the line
and it was hard to take, after their uncompromising attitude.
But the evidence was there—indisputable evidence—and the
enemy capitulated. Of course, some argument ensued about
the geological age of the deposit. Dr. Brown and several others
put it at the very close of the Ice Age, giving a date of about
twenty-five thousand years. Some geologists hesitated to go
that far. They preferred the early Recent period, allowing an
antiquity of from ten thousand to fifteen thousand years.

"Recent time," by the way, is determined in America by
the disappearance of the camel, horse, tapir, mammoth, giant
sloth, and some other mammals. But dating man's antiquity
by the extinction of his contemporary fauna, alone, yields no
certain results. Dr. Nelson tells me that the last time he talked
with Professor Scott of Princeton, he said he would not have
been surprised to learn that if Columbus had sailed up the
Hudson in 1492 he would have found mastodons browsing
on the west bank. If the earlier date for the Folsom points is
correct, as seems probable from later discoveries, the Folsom
people were in America during the Upper Old Stone Age
when Cro-Magnon man and his relatives occupied Central
and Western Europe. Moreover, before the end of the Ice
Age, man had wandered as far south as Patagonia, the extreme tip of South America.

Folsom Man, as an individual, remains a mystery. Not a single scrap of human bone has been found in any of the deposits. But the darts, now called "Folsom points," do tell an important story. They differ materially from any others in America or Europe, for that matter. The stone work is of a very high order. The points are about two inches long, thin and leaf-shaped with concave bases. The most distinctive feature is a longitudinal groove on either face, something like a modern bayonet, giving a greater penetrating power than that of an ordinary stone arrowhead. Probably they were not arrowheads at all, for it is unlikely that the Folsom people knew bows and arrows, which do not appear in European culture until the Late Palaeolithic in Spain and Mesolithic in the Baltic area. Spear throwers called "atlatls," however, were used, and the points appear to be tips for the lances. Their manufacture required a high degree of skill, so we may infer that Folsom Man was a pretty intelligent individual.

To the credit of American archaeologists be it said that most of the critics became enthusiastic converts and endorsed the fact that Folsom Man lived in America many thousands of years before the Shell Mound people and the Basket Makers. Moreover, an energetic search was inaugurated for other deposits. Museum collections were re-examined and unrecognized Folsom points appeared. In 1931 near Angus, Nebraska, a point was discovered associated with the bones of a long extinct elephant. Another was identified under the pelvis of a mammoth in northeastern Colorado, and New Mexico produced two important sites. Both of the latter were discovered by the late Dr. E. B. Howard, of the University of Pennsylvania

221

1942 EX. Bryn Mawr

Museum in Philadelphia. In the first, at Burnet Cave, near Carlsbad, a point lay buried beneath the Basket Maker culture and associated with the bones of a musk-ox-like animal which suggests that the climate was much colder at that time than it is today. Twenty-eight miles north of Fort Collins, Colorado, an important site—a deeply buried deposit—was found on land owned by Mr. William Lindermeier. Apparently Folsom men had rounded up a herd of nine bison (*Bison antiquus taylori*) and made a grand killing. They camped at the spot, barbecued the bison, and a camel as well. Charred bones, a few simple flint implements, some unfinished points and fireplaces suggest that they had lived there for some time. The fact that no ornaments or carvings of any kind were found indicates that these people were far less advanced than those of Magdalenian times at the end of the Old Stone Age in Europe, at least so far as art is concerned.

In a book of this character it would be futile to enumerate the many sites where Folsom points have been found. Yet I must mention that at Yuma, Colorado, delicately chipped stone points of a different type were discovered on the surface. These appear to be as old, if not older, than those of Folsom. Suffice it to say that at the very end of the Ice Age Folsom Man inhabited a wide area of western America east of the Rocky Mountains from Alberta and Saskatchewan and south to the Mexican border.

An energetic search for more information concerning these earliest Americans continues. Frank C. Hibben, formerly of the University of New Mexico, organized an expedition in 1941 to explore what he thought might be the migration route

of Folsom Man from Siberia. Careful questioning of sour-
doughs led the archaeologists along the coast of British Columbia and Alaska to Fairbanks. There, in a muck pit, only a
yard from the skeleton of an extinct Alaskan lion, they discovered a doubtful Yuma-like point still frozen securely in
the matrix, seventy-five feet below the present surface of the
valley.

A single point purchased in a curio store in Ketchikan,
Alaska, some years earlier had inspired Dr. Hibben to inau-
gurate the Alaskan search. He learned that the point had been
found originally by a man named Eagle Johnson, who, alas,
was dead. But a fisherman told them that Eagle had discovered
a quantity of flints and bones at Chinitna Bay. So there they
went. Almost immediately they located a bank far above the
normal high-tide mark from which projected bits of flint,
bones, and pieces of frozen wood. For a mile along the beach
the explorers followed the evidence, learning that, many thousands of years ago, early man of some kind had camped at
this very spot. They found charred mammoth bones, charcoal,
points, and chips from the stones used in their manufacture.
Eventually the archaeologists were driven out of the bay by
violent storms and high tides, but they plan to make another
expedition after the war.

While Dr. Hibben feels morally certain that the stone darts
he discovered are Folsom points, some other archaeologists
do not agree with him. Dr. N. C. Nelson believes that Hibben's
claim is not borne out by his published illustrations and the
identification of his so-called Yuma point is none too good.
The Eskimo in fairly recent times made slate points with

Folsom type flutings. Dr. Nelson says that at present it looks as though the Folsom technique was originated in America and never reached Asia. Only further material will demonstrate who is right.

Be that as it may, the search is not without hope of a spectacular result. As Dr. Hibben says, much of northern Alaska is blanketed with black silt, eternally frozen three feet below the surface. Many of the animal bones still retain traces of flesh, tendons, and scraps of skin. Hibben's party were even induced to sample the flesh of a mammoth. He remarks that it was "almost black, coarse grained, but apparently perfectly preserved. After rudimentary cooking it tasted very much as one would expect it to taste—like a combination of sand and mud. However, our Eskimo dogs seemed greatly to relish this ten thousand year old meat." (1944) Since some of the animals were preserved in cold storage, why not a man himself? The Berezovka Mammoth is a classic example of what one may expect to find in the eternally frozen North. That one of the earliest Americans may be discovered intact is by no means a vain hope.

Folsom Man was obviously an itinerant hunter depending entirely upon game. Doubtless he ate roots and berries, wild seeds and vegetation, but bison were his main food supply supplemented with mammoth and sometimes a camel and other game. There is no evidence that he cultivated grain or had any knowledge of drawing, painting, or sculpture, as did his Magdalenian contemporaries in Europe.

That the earliest inhabitants of America arrived here by way of Alaska seems almost certain. No other migration route is plausible. The "Lost Continent of Atlantis" as a stepping-stone from Europe to America has long been an intriguing popular theory. So also the "Lost Continent of Mu" (or Lemuria) in the Pacific where civilization first started, according to Colonel James Churchward. "Lost continents" and "lost civilizations" have always fired popular imagination. Probably they will continue to do so until the end of time, fed by the theories of occult groups who flourish all over the world. I suppose that in the last thirty years I have had a thousand letters inquiring whether Churchward's "Land of Mu" was fact or fiction. A good many, too, about Atlantis, although the literature on that subject, alone, numbers more than twenty-five thousand volumes. Intriguing as the theories are, they do not happen to be true. Continents have risen and sunk, land bridges were built and broken at various periods in geological history, and cities were buried beneath the desert sands. But all have left behind them indisputable proof of their existence. Atlantis and Mu do not bear the cold analysis of science.

Of course, the believers are not really interested in discovering how America was populated. Otherwise, they would simply look at the map and observe that Alaska and Asia are separated by not more than fifty-six miles of water, with islands between for steppingstones. They could be told, also, that for millions of years the gap between the two continents has not been wider than it is at present; that since the Upper Tertiary period the two continents have been more or less continually connected by a land bridge. Sometimes it was broad, and sometimes narrow, or broken, but it served as a corridor for the migration of animals and plants. A great many extinct animals were common to both continents, and our American big-horn sheep, so-called Rocky Mountain goat, moose, caribou, and other living animals are of undoubted Asiatic origin. They could see that within Bering Strait there are two rocky islands and that the longest stretch of open water is only twenty-five miles.

I stood one day on Cape Prince of Wales and looked across to Fairway Rock and the Diomedes. The weather was not very clear but I could see them distinctly, resting comfortably midway in the Strait. Primitive man doubtless looked many times from the opposite mainland to the spot where I was standing. With his inherent explorer's instinct, the new land was a constant challenge. How he first came to America is uncertain. It may be that he walked across on the land bridge. During the advanced stages of glaciation the ocean bed was supposed to have been raised or the sea level lowered sufficiently to make Bering Sea dry land. Possibly he came by boat. Even rude canoes would be able to traverse the narrow stretches of water with land continually in sight. Perhaps his first visit was by way of the ice. In Bering Strait the pack ice is usually in motion but farther to the north it would offer as easy travel as the land itself. Even during the end of the Ice Age the glaciers were restricted almost entirely to the mountains. None of them reached far into the lowlands fronting the coastal ranges, so that a large area was free of ice and offered a haven for animals and plants driven from the glaciated regions.

Because primitive man lived mostly on meat, it is easy to

understand why he followed the game, ever seeking new and richer hunting grounds. Probably the invasion of Alaska was first by small groups, then by greater numbers as news of the new world spread among distant residents. One can hardly conceive a "gold rush" such as that of the Klondike; more likely it was a slow infiltration extending over thousands of years. From just what region they came is a matter of speculation, but their physical resemblance suggests that the relatives of the early Americans may have come from as far south as Tibet. The migration route could well have been up the China coast, into Siberia and thence to Alaska. Southward the western slope of the Rocky Mountains offered an attractive path to our Southwest and to South America. Tracing the migration routes into and throughout America is a fascinating problem for future exploration.

Presumably it did not take many centuries for the ancestors of our American Indians to spread widely over their newly discovered continent. As they met different conditions of climate, food, and geography, each group adapted itself to its own particular environment and developed its own tribal characters and culture.

That our Indians are basically Mongoloid seems to be the accepted opinion among most anthropologists. That does not mean that the earliest Mongols were their direct ancestors. They were closely related to, and probably originated from, the same Central Asiatic stock which gave rise to the Chinese and other Mongoloid people. To the casual observer the similarity of the living Mongols and Tibetans to our Indians is remarkable. All of us on the Central Asiatic Expedition were impressed by the number of Mongols that resembled certain Indians as much as two peas in a pod. Moreover, their characteristics and habits are amazingly alike, although this is probably largely a matter of similar environment.

Reports of very ancient human remains in America, none of which could be verified beyond reasonable doubt, have been so frequent that in part it was responsible for the hard-boiled attitude of anthropologists. I have remarked that no bones of Folsom Man whatever have been recovered. Not a single scrap. This does not mean that they will not be found. I am firmly convinced that with post-war intensive exploration this "missing link" in American prehistory will be discovered.

But as the case stands today, the earliest authentic human remains in the new world come from South America. Junius Bird, an energetic and enthusiastic young archaeologist of the American Museum of Natural History, with his wife, discovered two caves in Patagonia where several human skeletons lay under earth and ashes with bones of the extinct sloth and American wild horse. Since the remains were on the original rock floors of the caves, and four culture periods lay above them, it is obvious they were the first inhabitants. The skulls resemble the long-headed type of certain American Indians. The upper incisor teeth are "shovel shaped," a practically universal characteristic of American Indians. It frequently occurs, also, in Chinese and Japanese, is rare among Negroes, and is virtually never found in Europeans. There is every reason to believe that these skeletons represent the ancestors of our living Indians; moreover, that all the early invasions from Asia have been of Mongoloid people.

The culture discovered by Bird appears to be not older than five thousand years, nor younger than thirty-five hundred. This leaves a wide gap between the time when Folsom Man first appeared fifteen to twenty-five thousand years ago. What happened during that long period? Did Folsom Man become extinct, leaving America uninhabited until a new migration of Mongoloids appeared with bows and arrows and domesticated dogs? It is a problem for the future explorer.

Unsuccessful attempts have been made to bridge the time gap, but only one find has resulted in arousing real interest among anthropologists. That is the so-called "Minnesota Man," or rather girl, discovered accidentally in 1931, near the town of Pelican Rapids, by road makers. She was fifteen years old at the time of her demise and some anthropologists maintain that she either fell, or jumped, into a glacier lake about twenty thousand years ago.

Professor A. A. Jenks of the University of Minnesota is her most ardent sponsor, and the late Dr. Ales Hrdlicka became her most vehement opponent. The poor little girl's skeleton was the cause of acid controversy, for the distinguished Hrdlicka was never one to fight a scientific battle with gloves on. He believed that she was only a Sioux Indian who had been buried not so very long ago in the glacial clay of Pelican Lake. Dr. Jenks would have none of that. Her tooth pattern and other characters, he said, "proclaim it to be a primitive *Homo sapiens,* of an early type of evolving Mongoloid, already prophetically suggesting American aborigines, especially the Eskimo."

Other anthropologists and geologists entered the fray, some

for, some against, the antiquity of the girl's remains. From the geological standpoint, the dispute centered about whether or not the grave was an intrusive burial long after the varved deposits had been laid down. The age of the clays themselves never was in doubt. The point is still unsettled, but not to have its claim to the oldest human remains in America rest merely on the slender bones of a girl, Minnesota has produced two other skeletons. One from Brown's Valley, near Fertile, and the other from Sauk Valley, West Union township. In both cases it is impossible to determine the age of the deposits with certainty, nor is it sure that the burials were not intrusive. In spite of the doubts, the finds cannot be dismissed as valueless. They would fit nicely into the picture of Folsom Man and we may have him without being willing to admit the fact, just as the "Red Lady of Paviland" became a Cro-Magnon man after nearly a century of delayed recognition.

CHAPTER FIFTEEN

Aftermath of the Old Stone Age

WITH THE CLOSE of the Old Stone Age and the establishment of Wise Man, this book ends, for it was intended to be an account only of early human evolution. It is then that the story of modern man, our own story, really begins. It is built upon the history of the past just as I built myself a modern house at Pondwood Farm upon the foundations of a colonial dwelling which stood upon this spot when America was young.

It carries through a transition period of stone culture called the Mesolithic, when human development seemed to retrogress before it entered the Neolithic or New Stone Age. Just what happened at the end of the Magdalenian period to cause this degeneration no one knows. But the fact remains that, at least in Europe, drawing, painting, and sculpture virtually disappeared and the making of bone and flint artifacts centered upon such small types that the period is sometimes referred to as the Microlithic. True, the climate and environment had radically altered. As the glaciers withdrew, the mammoth, woolly rhinoceros, and reindeer disappeared from Western Europe and the life and food of the resident humans changed. Instead of the virile hunting type fostered by the rigors of the chase after dangerous game, their culture degenerated into fishing, living on roots, native plants, and shellfish. No animals were domesticated except the dog. Extensive migrations of peoples seem to have taken place during this period, invasions coming into Europe from Africa and the East. It was an era of pause and readjustment preparatory to the great surge forward into the New Stone Age.

Dr. Raymond Murray rightly says that this period should more appropriately be named the "New Age" without reference to the stone industry, for it was primarily an age of social and economic revolution.

The discovery of nature's creative forces in the growing of plants and vegetables, the domestication of animals, the making of pottery and invention of weaving were far more significant than the development of polished stone implements from which the period takes its name. These were so good, however, that a Danish woodsman, using only stone axes, cut the timbers and built a house in eighty-one days.

Probably the earliest domestication of animals and plants did not originate in Europe but came there from Egypt and Mesopotamia or the desert highlands between Anatolia and the Indies. Agriculture made it possible for people to live together in large communities, or towns, to give up hunting as their chief occupation and to travel widely because food could be carried with them in their vessels, bags, and baskets. They developed real houses. Some of them were partly excavated in the earth and roofed with timbers and others built of wood in the open.

The most spectacular of all Neolithic villages were those discovered in the Swiss Lake region in 1853, when an especially low-water period in one lake brought to light the remains of dwellings built on piles. These dwellings were grouped together and told a fascinating story of Neolithic life. Wood had been utilized in a high degree for the making of bowls, cups, and spoons, and a variety of grains was cultivated. Barley, millet, peas, beans, lentils, and apples were part of their food, along with pigs, goats, and sheep.

In this period we see the beginning of trade, or commerce. Amber beads and other articles of personal adornment as well as unworked flint were taken considerable distances to be exchanged for other desiderata. By the time the New Stone Age ended man had spread over much of the habitable parts of the earth.

Then came the discovery of metals. It was only a few years ago, judged by the time-scale we have been considering in this book. A mere four or five thousand years when copper and bronze changed the world's civilization. The Egyptians as early as 5000 B.C. had used raw copper, iron, gold, and silver, beating out ornaments, but melting and casting them did not come until much later. Probably gold was the first metal discovered, but it was used only to make gew-gaws for personal adornment. The really precious metal was copper, which could be hammered into any desired shape and hardened somewhat during the process. Presumably, the fact that metal could be melted out of rock came by accident at the campfire. Dr. Breasted thinks this discovery was first made in the Sinai Peninsula about 4000 B.C. Where or when it was learned that

233

by the addition of tin, copper could be hardened into bronze, no one knows, but probably it was discovered in the Near East not long after copper had been first smelted. In parts of Europe, however, the Age of Copper and Bronze did not start until about 3000 B.C. Iron seems to have been used in India as early as 1400 B.C., but the Hittites were probably its first real developers. In China it had become so commonly used by 800 B.C. that a tax was levied upon its transportation.

After the Iron Age came the Age of Steel in which we are living today. What man has done in this latest era is a matter of written history. As to what he will do in the future, we can only speculate.

CHAPTER SIXTEEN

Man of the Future

HUMAN BEINGS, half a million years from now, would be caricatures in our eyes—something out of a bad dream. Big round heads, almost globular, hairless as a billiard ball, even the women! Very clever these future people will be—much more intelligent than we are, for their brains will be better developed—but alas, at the expense of hearing, tasting, seeing, and smelling. Their faces will be smaller than ours, actually, and in proportion to the swollen heads. Shortened jaws will carry only twenty-six teeth instead of thirty-two, for our annoying wisdom teeth will no longer be there. Likewise, two of our front teeth (lateral incisors) are doomed to disappear. The dental profession will have an enormous boom, for what teeth remain must have constant attention from early childhood. Shorter bodies are predicted, with longer legs and only four toes. But they will be taller than we are; not exactly giants, but probably several inches taller. No, they won't be attractive, judged by our standards.

We might hesitate to invite one of those future humans to

dinner, were he to appear now in advance of his time, except that his conversational brilliance would put the rest of us to shame. But he would have some physical advantages over us. No sinus trouble for him, even in the worst weather. In speaking of operations he'd never mention appendicitis. Nor would he be afflicted with hernia. And falling of the uterus would be unknown to his wife. No more would the man of the house complain of backache from shoveling snow, for he'd have a much stronger back than ours. And falling arches would be unknown.

Such predictions aren't pure guesswork. To a certain extent we can judge the future by the past. Everything I have so confidently stated is based on the known progress of human evolution. Before us is the visible evidence of fossil human skeletons, beginning with that of Java Ape-Man more than half a million years old, and progressing in a definite sequence up to the present day. We have every reason to believe that the development or reduction of the same physical characters will continue into the future. We can visualize some of those changes if we forget the paltry six thousand years of known civilization and think in terms of thousands of centuries. Half a million years is about the least we can figure on, if we are to see fundamental differences in the human body.

When we begin to assess what may happen in the future, we think first of the human posture, for it was super-important in his evolution. Man became erect; he cannot be more vertical but doubtless he will be taller. Records of the last fifty years, both in Europe and America, show a constant increase in average stature. Perhaps vitamins are responsible or progress in medical science and hygiene, or any one of half a dozen other possibilities. We wouldn't know. Nevertheless, it is a fact that the present generation on the average is 3.55 centimeters (1.37 inches) taller than their fathers; younger sons are taller than their elder brothers, and the fathers are taller than their fathers. But it is doubtful that we will ever become giants. As was noted before, nature tried that experiment once and evidently found it unprofitable. Enormous size was a liability in the past and I can see less reason why it should be an asset in the future.

That our hypothetical man will have a larger skull is a safe prediction. The human brain has constantly increased in size and complexity since the Java Ape-Man, and has consequently required a larger head. The size of the brain, however, does not always indicate its intellectual power. Nevertheless, the dictum that the bigger the brain the better the man has held good as a general rule throughout human evolution.

Since the average brain capacity of the Ape Man was only 870 cubic centimeters, and modern man boasts an average of 1350 c.c.. future man can be expected to have at least 1725 c.c. Such heads would not make them unduly conspicuous even today, for it is not unknown in our present generation. They ought to be super-intelligent, with bulging foreheads housing wonderful frontal lobes. Not only has the volume of the brain constantly increased through the ages, but the centers connected with thinking have been improved by folding and a denser accumulation of nerve cells and fibers. This, however, at the expense of the sense areas. But modern man has compensated for that by inventing tools to sharpen the senses, such as the telescope, hearing devices, etc.—all products of his better brain. That the skull of future man will have a shorter base and be round instead of long and narrow is almost certain, since that has been the tendency in human evolution for half a million years. A round skull gives more brain room than one that is long and narrow. Thus we may expect our remote descendants to have almost globular heads perched atop their spinal columns.

The Java Ape-Man had overhanging brows caused by a heavy bar of bone above the eyes, as did Peking Man, Rhodesian Man, and Neanderthal Man. By the time our own species, the "Wise Man," arrived upon the scene, the bar had been greatly reduced. Nevertheless, its rudiments still persist in our faces. Logically the men of the future will have almost smooth brows. "Women's features point the direction in which evolution moves," says Sir Arthur Keith. The smooth-browed condition has already been achieved by the female of our species. And how they love it! But we poor males have lagged far behind our wives. We have an inconsiderable swelling above the root of the nose; on either side of this protuberance, vestigial ridges of bone still remain. Thus, women are about half a million years ahead of men, at least in this respect. But they need not be too smug. If sex differences persist, females of the future will rejoice in an almost bulbous forehead like a newborn baby's by the time we men have reached their present condition of beauty.

Modern man is in a deplorable condition regarding his teeth. They are frequently twisted, impacted, and mal-erupted. Of course, our soft food and polite manner of eating are largely responsible, although there may be other contributing causes. The Eskimos, who gnaw their bones, have beautiful teeth. So did most primitive men. You can't have good teeth or jaws unless you eat resistant food. We don't do it. If the time ever comes when man lives on concentrated food pills, he can say good-by to what is left of his teeth.

The earliest humans had long jaws and projecting faces. These have progressively shortened and receded as men climbed up the evolutionary ladder toward the modern type. Less use of the jaws and powerful chewing muscles enclosed by the cheekbones is largely responsible. Inevitably this will continue unless our eating habits change, and the hypothetical man will have a pitifully small and receding face.

Head and body hair is bound to go. There is nothing we can do about it. The man of the future will be lucky if his head does not resemble the surface of a billiard ball before he is thirty years old. No hope for the women either. Hair-do parlors will have little place in feminine life half a million years from now. Wig makers, yes, if that happens to be the style, but natural tresses will be a thing of the past. Body hair, too, will disappear. In the course of human evolution the pelt has constantly diminished. We do not need hair to keep us warm when clothes do the job. The yellow and black races already have lost most of their body hair. In that respect they are further advanced than their white relatives. It is true, also, that early baldness occurs much more frequently in highly civilized races than among primitive people. I never saw a bald Indian, Mongol, or South Sea Islander. But sit in the gallery of any theater of Europe or America and look down upon the shiny pates of half the men! That tells the story. Depilatory creams for the future feminine contingent will be unknown.

Our hypothetical man of the future will escape some of the ills that make our lives miserable. When we became bi-pedal vertical creatures our bodies necessarily went through a profound readjustment. Nature accomplished miracles in a short time but she left us with many weak spots, reminiscent of the haste with which she brought us upright. All our internal organs had to be suspended in the thorax or bound to the back wall; otherwise, they would sag distressingly. This necessitated a widening and flattening of the chest, and a great expansion of the pelvis to form a weight-bearing basin. Nevertheless, we are still poorly fitted mechanically for an upright posture. No automobile manufacturer would dare put a car on the market with so many defects.

In the first place, our chassis is much too long. It gives us a weak lower back. Few men reach middle life without aches and pains in the lumbar region. Since we have no support from the front legs the "small of the back" must bear the weight of the entire upper body. No wonder we have sacroiliac displacement! But nature is not one to let such a defect in architecture go on indefinitely. Obviously, our backs must be shortened or strengthened. Either we must lose a lumbar vertebra or the last one must be fused with the sacrum. Probably the latter will happen.

Our abdominal protuberance, embonpoint, is another weak spot. The curve of the lumbar vertebrae pushes the abdomen forward between the ribs and the pelvis in a decidedly unlovely and mechanically imperfect manner. Therefore men get hernia and women prolapsed uterus. These ills should be much less prevalent when the back is shorter.

The hypothetical humans will not be troubled with an appendix for it is definitely on the way out. Moreover, nature is pretty certain to do something about our sinus afflictions. In the four-footed stage, the sinuses drained beautifully, but not so when we became vertical. The openings must migrate downward to function properly and they doubtless will do so.

The change in our extremities was a pretty good job on the whole. I doubt if our hands will alter much, but there is room for improvement in our feet. We still suffer from fallen arches, and that is pretty sure to be remedied. As the line of leverage in walking shifted from the middle to the big toe in modern man, the little toe became less and less important, until now it is almost useless and sometimes lacks a nail. Useless parts seldom persist indefinitely, so we can confidently predict that it is doomed to disappearance. As a matter of fact, we find plenty of precedent for the loss of toes in lower animals. The earliest known horse had four toes and now functions with only one. The cow, pig, and camel suffered a similar loss in pedal digits.

Such is an impressionistic picture of the future human so far as his physique is concerned. There we are on fairly safe ground, for his bodily development is bound to follow natural laws even though they are modified to some extent by our unnatural life in civilization. Of what will happen to him mentally and spiritually we can only guess. Dr. Harry Shapiro, from whom I have drawn many ideas embodied in this article is an optimist. He says: "Inevitably in the course of this long period of time civilizations will have declined and new ones will have arisen to take the lead for a time. Perhaps on several occasions civilization will come perilously near to barbarity, but it will ever spring anew to dizzier heights. There is nothing in human history inconsistent with this view." (1933, p. 584)

But the pessimist is entitled to his opinion. Drawing a picture of the hypothetical man of the future may have been a waste of thought. The human species may not continue to exist for another half million years. With his wonderful brain man may destroy himself. Each year he masters more of nature's forces. They enable him to fly in the air like the birds; to travel beneath the sea as do the whales and fishes; to talk without wires to the ends of the earth.

Throughout written human history wars have marched hand in hand with civilization. Every day man develops new and more terrible engines with which to destroy his own kind and the fruit of his labor. Within the life of the present generation, no place on the globe will be safe from his bombs and rockets. In a matter of minutes a whole city could be reduced to a heap of rubble and its inhabitants become nothing but charred and blackened bones. Only a few isolated humans might remain alive. It is not only possible, but highly probable, that the human race could not survive another war, without being mortally injured. Regardless of the possibility that man may destroy himself, the life cycle of all organic forms seems to be determined by nature. When they have lived their allotted span they disappear. Animal dynasties that have reached majestic heights now are known only from their fossilized remains. Palaeontologists speculate as to why they died but it is only speculation. Man's history on earth has been incredibly short and brilliant. Like a meteor flashing across the sky he has risen to control the animate world, but he may burn out as rapidly as that same shooting star, leaving behind only the dead records of his once glorious past.

BIBLIOGRAPHY

Abbot, C. G.
>1930 *Man from the Fartherest Past.* Smith. Sc. Series, Vol. 7.

Absolon, Karl
>1925 *Ill. Lond. News,* Oct. 31, Nov. 7, Nov. 14.
>1926 *Cent. European Observer,* Prague, Jan. 22, Vol. IV, No. 4.
>1929 *Ill. Lond. News,* Nov. 23, Nov. 30.

Akeley, Carl
>1923 *In Brightest Africa.* Doubleday, Doran & Co., Inc., Garden City, N. Y., 1923, p. 232.

Black, Davidson
>1933 "Fossil Man in China." Mem. Geol. Surv. Series A, No. 11, Peiping.
>1933ª "On the Discovery, Morphology and Environment of *Sinanthropus pekinensis.*" Phil. Trans. Roy. Soc. London, Ser. B, Vol. 223, pp. 57-120.

Broom, Robert
>1937 "On *Australopithecus* and its Affinities." *Early Man: International Symposium.* Acad. Nat. Sc., Phil., March, pp. 285-92.

Burkett, M. C.

1925 *Ill. London News,* Nov. 21.

Chaney, Ralph

1935 "The Food of Peking Man." Carnegie Inst. News
Serv. Bull. Vol. III, No. 25.

Dorsey, Geo. A.

1931 *Man's Own Show: Civilization.* Harper and Bros.,
New York and London.

Gregory, W. K.

1938 "Evidence of the Australopithecine Man-Apes on
the Origin of Man." *Science,* Dec. 30, 1938, Vol. 88,
No. 2296, pp. 615-16.

1939 "The Bearing of Dr. Broom's and Dr. Dart's Discoveries on the Origin of Man." *The Annual Pro-
ceedings, 1938-39,* The Assoc. Sc. & Tech. Socs. of S.
Africa, Kelvin House, Johannesburg, May, p. 45.

Gregory, W. K. and Hellman, Milo

1939 "The South African Fossil Man-Apes and the
Origin of the Human Dentition." *Jour. Am. Dental
Assoc.,* Vol. 26, pp. 558-64.

1939[a] "The Dentition of the Extinct South African Man-
Ape, *Australopithecus (Plesianthropus) transvaal-
ensis* Broom." A Comparative and Phylogenetic
Study. *An. Transvaal Mus.,* Vol. XIX, pt. 4, 1939.

1940 "The upper dental arch of *Plesianthropus transvaalensis* Broom and its relations to other parts of the
skull." *Am. Jour. Phys. Anthrop.,* Vol. 26, Mar. 30,
pp. 211-24.

Hibben, F. C.

    1944 "Our Search for the Earliest Americans." *Reader's Digest*, Sept. 1944, p. 15.

Hooton, E. A.

    1936 *Up from the Ape*. Macmillan Co., New York.

    1937 *Apes, Men, and Morons*. G. P. Putnam's Sons, New York.

Howells, William

    1944 *Mankind So Far*. Doubleday, Doran & Co., Inc., New York.

Hrdlicka, Ales

    1930 Smith. Sc. Ser. Vol. VII, p. 148.

    1930^a "The Skeletal Remains of Early Man." Smith. Misc. Col. Vol. 83, July 24, 1930.

Keith, Sir Arthur

    1931 *New Discoveries Relating to the Antiquity of Man*. W. W. Norton & Co., Inc., New York.

    1937 *Early Man* (in). Acad. Nat. Sc., Phil.

Koenigswald, G. H. R. von

    1937 "A Review of the Stratigraphy of Java and Its Relation to Early Man." *Early Man*. Acad. Nat. Sc., Phil.

    1940 "The South African Man-Apes and *Pithecanthropus*." Carnegie Inst. Wash. Pub. 530, pp. 205-22.

Matthew, W. D.

    1915 "Climate and Evolution." *An. N. Y. Acad. Sc.*, Vol. XXIV, Feb. 1915, pp. 209-10.

Murray, Raymond

    1943 *Man's Unknown Ancestors*. The Bruce Pub. Co., Milwaukee, Wis.

Nelson, N. C.

   1937 "Notes on the Cultural Relations between Asia and America." *Am. Antiquity,* Vol. 2, No. 4, Apr. 1937, pp. 267-72.

˜sborn, H. F.

   1918 *Men of the Old Stone Age.* Chas. Scribner's Sons, New York.

   1927 *Man Rises to Parnassus.* Princeton Univ. Press, Princeton, N. J.

Reeds, C. A.

   1931 *The Earth: Our Ever Changing Planet.* The Univ. Series, New York.

Shapiro, H. L.

   1933 "Man—500,000 Years from Now." *Natural History,* Vol. XXXIII, No. 6.

Smith, Sir G. Elliot

   1933 "Preliminary Report on the Cranial Cast." *Quart. Jour. Geol. Soc.,* Vol. 99, p. 147.

Shaafhausen, D.

   1857 *Verhandl. d. Naturhist.* Vol. 14, Bonn.

Saur, C. O.

   1944 "A Geographic Sketch of Early Man in America." *The Geog. Review,* Vol. XXXIV, No. 4, 1944, pp. 529-73.

Terra, Hellmut de

   1937 "The Siwaliks of India and Early Man." *Early Man.* Acad. Nat. Sc., Phil. 1937.

Tilney, Frederick

    1933 *The Master of Destiny*. Doubleday, Doran & Co., New York.

Weidenreich, Franz

    1938-39 "On the Earliest Representative of Modern Mankind Recovered on the Soil of East Asia." *Pk. Nat. Hist. Bull.*, 1938-39, Vol. 13, pt. 3, pp. 161-74.

    1938-39[a] "The Drift of Human Phylogenetic Evolution." *Pk. Nat. Hist. Bull.*, 1938-39, Vol. 13, pt. 4, p. 227.

    1940 "Man or Ape." *Nat. Hist. Mag.*, Vol. XLV, No. 1, Jan., pp. 32-37.

    1941 "Extremity Bones of *Sinanthropus pekinensis*." *Pal. Sinica*, New Ser. D. No. 5, Whole Ser. No. 116, pp. 1-150.

    1942 "Early Man in Indonesia." *Far Eastern Quarterly*, Nov., pp. 58-65.

    1943 "The Skull of *Sinanthropus pekinensis*." *Pal. Sinica*, New Ser. D. No. 10, Whole Series. 127, Dec. 1943.

    1944 "Giant Early Man from Java and South China." *Science*, June 16, 1944, Vol. 99, No. 2581, pp. 479-82.

248

INDEX

249

GORILLA

ORANGUTAN

SOME LIVING
MONGOLOIDS
(Homo sapiens)

CHIMPANZEE

PEKING
WOMAN

GIBBON

GIANTS
OF SOUTH
CHINA AND
JAVA

SOUTHERN
APE

THE FAMILY TREE
OF MAN

keep